PRAISE FOR A

'I first knew Mick in 1970 when he joined Newmarket's cricket tour to the Lake District. He subsequently joined the club shortly afterwards when the club ceased playing friendlies to join the Suffolk League. He became captain after only one year, and, under his inspiring captaincy, led the club to many cup successes, culminating in winning the Suffolk League in 1977.

'Energy and persistence to conquer anything' is a phrase that sums Mick up, hence his many achievements in sport, business, and in his personal life, since those unforgettable days.

His book is a most enjoyable read for all!'

Keith White – Newmarket, Suffolk

'I have known Mick since we were teenagers; we grew up in neighbouring villages. Cricket and football were very important to our social and mental wellbeing. I followed the sports with much interest, and Mick was very talented at both. After being friends at Cheveley School, we travelled daily together by steam train from Newmarket to Cambridge Technical College from 1958–59 to further our education. Afterwards, we both went our separate ways, and got married. Mick, being very motivated and ambitious, settled in Scotland with his family. We rekindled our friendship after we were both widowed and continue to visit each other to this day.

As an ordinary village lad, Mick's many successes in sport and business detailed in his book are an inspiration to all.'

Pauline Burningham – Ashley, Cambridgeshire

'I first knew Mick when he was appointed as RMA for Barclays Life Manchester in 1980. He proved early on to be very capable when set difficult challenges.

I have admired him over the years: from a business perspective, sport, and as a friend. We have remained friends for 45 years. He not only gave me self-confidence and belief in myself, but also in the team he built in Scotland when he formed his own company. I was privileged to be part of that team.

Sport, especially cricket, was his main passion, to which he showed the same dedication and desire to succeed.

His journey from an ordinary working-class, village lad in 1943, to MD of one of Scotland's successful financial services companies, is mind-blowing.'

Jean Band – Alva, Clackmannanshire

A
CHEVELEY
LAD

MICHAEL JOHN HARRY NASH

First published 2025 by Wrate's Publishing

ISBN 978-1-917970-06-8

Copyright © Michael John Harry Nash

Edited and typeset by Wrate's Editing Services
www.wrateseditingservices.co.uk

The right of Michael John Harry Nash to be identified as the author of
this work has been asserted in accordance with the
Copyright, Designs and Patents Act, 1988.

A CIP catalogue record for this book is available from
the British Library.

The book is dedicated to my parents, who taught me right from wrong and never to waste anything.

To my wife Kate, to whom I was married for fifty-six happy years, and who was always an inspiration and support in everything I did.

Contents

1

EARLY DAYS

I was born on 31 January 1943, during the Second World War, at Broad Green, Cheveley, a village in Cambridgeshire, the nearest town being Newmarket in the county of Suffolk. My earliest memory, though very faint, was of my mother rushing to hide with me under a marble washstand in a bedroom as German bombers sounded overhead. When I was older, she told me she could identify the German bombers by the hum of their engines. They made a noise akin to the words 'I'm-a-coming, I'm-a-coming, I'm-a-coming'. This recognition came about as the German aircraft frequently passed over my parents' house on their bombing runs to factories in the Midlands.

As well as this wartime memory, Mum told me about two other incidents: one, the bombing of Newmarket High Street in February 1941 when she was due to go shopping, and the second in 1944, when a Stirling four-engine bomber crashed into some cottages at Broad Green, near to where my parents lived, soon after takeoff.

My parents were married in July 1940. Shortly after, my dad volunteered to join the Royal Air Force. He became a leading aircraftsman (LAC). As a member of the ground crew stationed at various bases around East Anglia, he helped to repair the bombers and fighter planes after they returned from action.

My mother, the second youngest of 15 children, volunteered for war work and gained employment at Burmetals, a factory near Birmingham. She once described how she stood on a hill in the city with others and watched the destruction of Coventry by German bombers.

Being a war baby, I have no major recollections of this time other than what my parents have told me, but I do appreciate what a challenging period 1939–1945 must have been for them; for everyone. The future was so uncertain, especially for people living in London who, night after night, were subjected to mass bombing raids by the German Luftwaffe. These raids became known as The Blitz.

I admire everyone who survived those years. We must never forget that freedom is not free.

I was aged two years and four months when the war ended on 8 May 1945, Germany finally surrendering. Mum and Dad looked forward to a better future as Dad resumed his previous occupation of working in the horse racing industry. He was successful in his application for the position of stallion man at the Great Barton Stud, situated just outside Bury St. Edmunds. The stud was owned by Lord Fairhaven, and the Aga Khan's stallions were stabled there.

We lived in a house at the bottom of the rear drive leading to the main stud – 1 Barton Stud Cottage. The house was detached and had three bedrooms, a kitchen, living room, front room and a pantry. It had electricity but no inside toilet nor hot water. The toilet was a small brick extension attached to the house at the side, so you had to go outside to access it. The actual toilet was an Elsan, which had a conventional toilet seat with lid, but underneath was a metal bucket that had to be emptied. With no running hot water, we had to boil kettles or saucepans on oil stoves. This meant that daily washing was confined to hands, face, and feet in the kitchen sink. Every fortnight, a long metal bath was brought out and placed on the kitchen floor, half filled with hot water. This was bath night.

The garden was quite large, with some fruit trees and an area that was fenced off with wire to contain several ducks. I enjoyed being asked to collect the eggs. Unlike chickens, ducks lay their eggs among nettles and patches of grass, so searching for them was a challenge. My dad grew lots of vegetables, and the duck eggs, when plentiful, were preserved in isinglass in a metal bucket for use when they were not.

Each year, the men working on the stud were given half a pig by the owner, which was then cut into joints and preserved in salt in a wooden barrel until needed. Milk was also supplied daily from the stud farm cows, which had to be collected. Trees surrounded the property on three sides and the back garden overlooked a corn field. It was a dream for a boy like me to grow up with so much space to roam and discover.

My earliest memory of Great Barton was of my paternal grandfather, William Trott, staying with us and going for a walk with me in my pushchair to the village of Great Barton, about three miles distant. On the way, I remember him parking the pushchair and wedging a piece of stick in the wheel to stop it from running away as the brake was not working. Other than that incident, I do not remember very much of my grandfather, who died on 8 July 1947, aged 74. As for my grandmother, Florence Trott (née Barrow), she died before I was born – 12 January 1941, aged 65.

On 6 November 1945, my brother Dennis was born. Around the same time, I discovered the children of our nearest neighbours, Danny and Freda Alcock. They lived in a thatched cottage immediately across the drive. They had a boy named Raymond and a girl called Janie. Raymond was the same age as me and Janie the same as my brother.

After Easter 1948, at the age of five, I started school. I attended Great Barton Primary, a Church of England school. On my first day, Mum took me on her bicycle, which had a child's seat mounted on the back made from a type of wicker. A memory of my first day was of playing with a wooden train set with a boy called Alan Mills. The other vivid memory is learning the alphabet by writing with a piece of chalk on a black slate. The classroom had very colourful biblical pictures on all the walls, and each morning we had assembly and prayers. Midway through the morning, we were provided with a half-pint bottle of milk to drink during what was known as playtime. Some children were given a spoonful of malt extract. This, I learned later, was for children who were considered undernourished and needed building up after the lean war years when food was scarce.

My journey to school was made twice a day, a three-and-a-half-mile round trip. I was collected and brought home for lunch, usually by Dad, and then taken back again for afternoon lessons. It was fortunate that my parents could share this duty. My dad had flexible working hours, looking after the two stallions stabled in the yard adjacent to our house. Eventually, however, I stayed for school dinners.

The school grounds were partly wooded, so, as well as the usual football and cricket games, during playtime there were all sorts of other games in which to participate. On one occasion, I decided to aggravate a wasps' nest in the hedge by poking it with a stick. I was stung several times and had to be taken home. Mum applied a 'blue bag' on the stings. This blue bag was intended for laundry use – to whiten clothes – but it was also believed the alkaline would remedy wasp stings.

Two years later, my brother, Dennis, started school. Each morning, he and I, together with Raymond and Janie (the neighbours' children) would walk down the avenue to the main road, catch the local bus to the village, then walk the last half a mile to school. The bus fare cost 1d. Sometimes, we would deliberately miss the bus and walk/run the entire way – three-and-a-half miles. This meant that after school, we could go to the village shop and spend the money on sweets, which were still rationed, eating them on the walk home. Most days in the summer we did walk both ways, looking for birds' nests. We always stopped in a field that had large, ancient oak trees. These trees had hollow trunks, and branches where jackdaws and owls would nest. We would put our hands into the holes of the trees to check for eggs and then take one for our collection (if it was a type we didn't already have).

Before collecting birds' eggs became illegal, we would go 'bird nesting' during the long, hot summer holidays. This was considered a hobby in those days. We got to know the varied species of birds and understood the habitats of many. Ponds were plentiful and usually had a moorhen's nest in the middle. We devised a way of taking an egg by tying a spoon to a long piece of stick, then reaching out to the nest to lift it out, all while being held so as not to fall in the water! The eggs of jackdaws we'd find in the holes of trees, were extracted in a similar way if we couldn't reach to grab an egg by hand. Having stolen the egg, the skill was then to climb back down the tree without breaking it. Providing the egg wasn't too big, one technique was to put it inside your mouth, but if it broke, then you had to spit out raw egg. Once safely home, the eggs were 'blown' to get out the yolk and white, otherwise they would rot. This was achieved by pricking both ends with a pin, blowing from one end so the yolk and white came out the other. We were always careful not to take eggs that had started to turn into embryos or were ready for hatching – the weight of the egg was the deciding factor.

During the school holidays, there would be the opportunity for at least a couple of daytrips to the seaside. Such excursions were typically organised by Mulley's, a coach firm from Bury St. Edmunds, that would collect people from the nearby villages. These trips had to be prebooked – Clacton-on-Sea, Great Yarmouth, and Felixstowe, the nearest coastal resorts. This was something I looked forward to as it was the only time we were able to see the seaside. On one such trip, I went into the sea for a paddle and stood on some broken glass. I had to visit the first aid tent to have my foot bandaged!

Living in the countryside, school holidays were an amazing time, especially during the summer when the days always seemed hot and sunny. Together with the Alcock children, Dennis and I would be outside most of the day, roaming all over the surrounding fields and woods, discovering nature. As well as 'bird nesting', collecting car numbers, matchbox labels, and cigarette packets were other hobbies which kept us occupied, and we'd constantly check the verges along the main road to Bury St. Edmunds in search of them. There were very few cars on the roads, so we were never in any danger of being run over. Still, we kept to the verges. Compared to the overprotective society of today, we never felt the need to be cautious; we had a freedom of which children nowadays can only dream.

We did, however, have some escapades, two that I especially remember. The first was trekking across the fields to a railway crossing called Catishall Gates, a line that passed over a minor country road. A few minutes before a train's arrival, the gatekeeper had to leave his signal box at the crossing junction to close the gates to passing traffic. After the gates were closed and the gatekeeper had returned to his signal box, we would sneak up to the line and lay pennies on the top of the rail, so they would get flattened as the train passed over them.

The other escapade occurred in a nearby meadow, where large, hollow tree trunks lay after being felled many years prior. We'd crawl inside and use them as houses, eating the bread and cakes we'd taken from the pantry at home. One day, someone had brought some matches and thought it would be a good idea to have a little fire inside the hollow tree as we played. It turned to evening, so we returned home to bed, extinguishing the fire before we left. Or so we'd thought. The next day, we discovered that the huge trunk had burned, now just a smouldering pile of ash. The fire we thought we had put out had remained alight, fanned by the wind, consuming the entire tree. Our parents told us that people had reported it burning during the night, but as it was ablaze in an open field with no threat to property or life, it was left to burn. No one could explain how it caught fire, and we never did confess.

As we grew older, ball games, particularly cricket and football, featured highly. I'd play in the garden with Dennis, Raymond and Janie. Cricket stumps were made of sticks pulled from hedges, and a bat was made by Dad from a piece of discarded fence rail which surrounded the stud paddocks. This may well have been the start of my long association with cricket. I would spend hours throwing a tennis ball up against the wall of the house to practice catching or returning it with the homemade bat as it came back at different heights and angles. At the age of eight, I was selected from my junior school to play for Great Barton Senior School against another school team on the playing fields of Great Barton. I was the only one chosen, and all the other team members were much older than me. Though I did not bat nor bowl, I enjoyed my first experience of being part of a team.

Having featured in the school's squad, I was then asked by Robin Hopwood, whose father was the stud groom at Barton Stud, to play in his team. Robin organised the group to play against other local teams on one of the stud paddocks. A proper grass pitch was prepared, and stumps pitched, with matching bails made from hazel sticks cut from a hedge. I batted at number 10 and scored two runs off a leg glance and bowled an over. Robin's grandfather saw me play. He said I had a wonderful left arm action and could one day play for England!

Spring was the time to search for baby rabbits. We would find warrens and push a stick down them. If we found fur on the end when we pulled it out, it indicated a nest inside. We would then monitor it. When the baby rabbits were about three weeks old, we would remove them and take them home, where we'd feed them milk and keep them as pets.

Once, we found a baby pigeon that had fallen out of its nest. We took it home and fed it until it was strong enough to fly. It did, however, get out of the cage one day, where it remained out of reach in a nearby tree. All attempts to get it down failed, so my father and friends threw lumps of soil at it until eventually it was knocked down. Fortunately, it was not hurt, and I was able to put it back in the cage and keep it as a pet. Later, I let it go.

We always looked forward to harvest time as this was when the surrounding fields of corn, wheat, oats and barley were cut with a machine called a binder which was towed by a tractor. Firstly, the binder cut the standing corn. This was then knocked down into a conveyor belt and carried to a device that tied it into a bundle, known as a sheaf. It was then ejected onto the harvested field, ready to be gathered by the farmhands before being then stood on end to dry. We would hide within the stooks so our parents could not find us; eating a picnic of bread and jam out of sight. We each had a claim to a particular field and named it after ourselves. The farmworkers got to know us and were very friendly; we even had our own favourite tractor driver who we laid claim to as well.

Just before Christmas 1949, I was collected from Cheveley by my uncle Will and Auntie Florrie. My uncle was stud groom at Warren Stud, and I went to stay with them and my cousin Derek until my sister was born on 7 January 1950. During this time, I helped on the stud, collecting the hens' eggs and helping to feed the horses and cows. I was even given a small wage packet each week when the men were paid.

For Christmas, I was given a toy crane which became one of my favourite toys. It had a pulley that worked the hook and another that lowered or raised the arm. Auntie Florrie would ask me to stand on a chair and sing 'Away in a manger' when visitors came, as she thought I had a lovely voice.

I don't remember much more of my holiday with them, apart from my cousin, Derek. He had a small, model steam engine that worked just like the real thing. (Until the mid-1950s, when the modern tractors were introduced, steam engines were used extensively in farming, especially for threshing and ploughing.) I was so fascinated with Derek's engine, my auntie Florrie promised I could have it when I was a bit older. However, despite seeing it many times over the following years, it was never given to me. One day during that initial stay with my aunt and uncle, Derek came home after playing football with friends. He was told off for being wet and dirty, and he wasn't allowed out to play the next time he asked. It was during my stay there that, for the first time, I washed in a porcelain bath where hot water came out of a tap.

I was back at home one week after Christmas to see my baby sister, Gillian Freda Ann, who had been born whilst I was away. I went back to school learning more words and numbers – I recall having to stand on a chair and a nurse checking my hair for headlice. Some children went to see the visiting school dentist. This was scary as they returned to the class with a plaster across their mouths, presumably because they had had teeth pulled out.

After the school summer holidays of 1950, I was moved up to Mrs Reeves' junior class where there were more subjects to be learned, such as English, arithmetic and geography. The school reports of 1951 and 1952, which I still have, indicate I did well. I was fully prepared for senior school in September 1952, when suddenly my schooling at Great Barton ended. My dad had decided to change jobs, the Great Barton Stud no longer keeping stallions. It being his main duty, this meant if he wanted to stay, he would have to revert to an ordinary stud hand with less pay. Dad had applied for a job as stallion man at Sandwich Stud in the village of Cheveley, just outside Newmarket, which he got. My mother had always wanted to return to Cheveley where they were both born and where two of her sisters still lived with their families; so too Dad's younger brother. So, in early September 1952, a furniture van pulled up outside our house, into which we loaded all our possessions, and set off for Cheveley.

2

CHEVELEY

We were due to move into a brand-new house on the Sandwich Stud estate, but the building work was behind schedule. As my dad needed to start his new job, Mum's older sister, Dora, found us a temporary terraced house. It was originally only supposed to be our home for one month, but it turned out to be three. It was an end terrace, one of four owned by Mr Dellar. It had a corrugated tin roof and no running water or electricity, and the toilet was in the back yard. The water had to be fetched from the village pump on the main street, while light was provided by oil lamps and candles. The front door opened into the only living room, and then through to the kitchen. The stairs were steep and narrow, leading to the two bedrooms. At night, you could hear the rats and mice scampering along the roof and the walls, which were only lathe and plaster. Despite all of this, Mum coped well and made it a comfortable, cosy home.

This temporary home had one distinct advantage: it was opposite the Cheveley recreation ground, where Cheveley Football Club played. They were a successful side, competing in the Bury and District Leagues. I supported them at home matches and sometimes at away matches too, travelling on the bus with the team. Every day after school, the local boys, which included my schoolfriends, and cousins Derek Hicks, and Neville and John Godfrey, would meet at the recreation ground for a kickabout until it was bedtime. I got lots of football practice.

On the first day of the school term, Mum took Dennis and I to register at the junior school. There, we met the headmaster, Hubert Parker Moore, known as 'Chick' Moore. He had taught my mother in 1932, so it was an interesting meeting for them both, reconnecting after 20 years. My brother Dennis, now aged six, was placed in the infants' class, taught by Mrs Walters, and I was placed in the juniors' class under Miss Nevard. Miss Nevard was a very tall teacher who wore glasses. Though quite strict, she taught well. I sat next to a girl called Vivienne Cornwall who lived in one of the prefabricated buildings at the other end of the village. These were homes for those who worked at a radio station complex, of which her father was one. Vivienne was nice, the first girl I was aware of being attracted to. Her best friend was Janet Pope, whom I later learned liked me!

As well as being an infants' school, Cheveley CofE was also a junior catchment area for other villages, which included Ashley, Kirtling, Upend, Woodditton, and Saxon Street. The youngest of these pupils were brought in by taxi, while the older ones cycled.

Mum's ambition was to have Christmas dinner in our new house, which we did. This was due to her constantly chivvying up the builders every time she paid them a visit to see what had been done. Each time we visited the property to monitor progress, something was usually brought from our temporary house, such as a spare chair. Such things had to be carried half a mile to the new house. Just before Christmas 1952, we finally moved into 1 Sandwich Stud Cottages.

Life at Cheveley CofE School was enjoyable, and my brother and I soon fitted in and made lots of friends. Jimmy Ranner, a boy who lived with his grandparents, became my best friend. We would often go off together after school in search of birds' eggs or to explore the fields and woods.

Mr Moore, the headmaster, was keen on sport. Depending on the time of year, every Wednesday afternoon either football or cricket was played at the recreation ground, which was just a five-minute walk from the school. Two boys would be nominated as captains and then take turns picking a player for their team from the rest of the class. Mr Moore would function as referee or umpire, occasionally taking off his jacket and playing as well.

We were taught all the standard subjects, such as arithmetic, English, history and geography. In addition, we learnt gardening – Mr Moore was a keen and knowledgeable gardener. The school had a large garden wherein grew many varieties of fruits and vegetables. One afternoon a week, boys in the senior class would be given tasks, working on different plots digging, planting, pruning or grafting, depending on the season. This would all be planned out in the classroom during the winter months when the weather prevented outside work. Every plot was carefully numbered, and the rows labelled, and we learnt the importance of crop rotation. It was such a successful garden, that it won the competition for the Best School Garden in Cambridgeshire. Chick Moore was immensely proud of the award and celebrated by buying everyone crates of Tizer and lemonade.

Whilst the boys were learning about gardening, the girls were taught domestic science, learning how to cook and do domestic tasks. Occasionally, there would be a swap, the boys spending a day in the domestic science room while the girls gardened. To this day, I still use gardening techniques I learnt at Cheveley CofE School, especially the importance of crop rotation to maximise the soil and prevent diseases.

With the sudden death of King George VI in 1952, in June 1953, the coronation of Queen Elizabeth II took place. Along with every other community in the UK, Cheveley village prepared to celebrate this occasion. There were lots of events planned at the recreation ground, but unfortunately it rained, so Britannia Hall, the local village hall, became the main centre of activity. I received a coronation mug and a brand-new half a crown, dated 1953, these distributed to every child.

After two years in Miss Nevard's class, I was moved into Mr Moore's class. I enjoyed his teaching as he made every subject interesting. He was also strict and occasionally used the cane. The misbehaving pupil would be caned on the hand in front of the class. Once, I was given the cane with Jimmy Ranner after we were accused of fighting in the playground.

Mr Moore was very keen on following cricket, so, in the summer, during the school lunchbreak from 12.30–1.30pm, he would switch on the school wireless to hear the Test match commentary. Those pupils keen on cricket could then listen to the last of the morning session live from Lords, Old Trafford, or one of the other Test match grounds. In those days, the Test matches started at 11.30am, so the first session ended at 1.30pm (unlike today when it ends at 1pm). If the commentary continued past 1.30pm, Mr Moore would wait until the last over had been completed before ringing the bell to signal the start of afternoon classes. This was sometimes as late as 1.40pm.

The nearest swimming pool was at Newmarket, so, during the summer term, a bus was provided for pupils who wanted to learn to swim. Once at the pool, we changed into swimming costumes for an hour's lesson. I went several times, but could not get the hang of the breaststroke, the stroke being taught. I never really learnt to swim then, like a lot of others did, though some pupils just went on the trip in preference to remaining at school. One morning, a boy from the village of Ashley, named Harold Jackson, got his arm wedged in the grab rail that ran around the edge of the pool and the fire service had to free him. This was done by using an axe to smash the rail so his arm could slide out. It was past lunchtime before we returned to school that day.

During breaktimes, we played cigarette card games, which were incredibly competitive. Cigarette cards first appeared in the UK in 1887. They were introduced to stiffen cigarette packets, as well as being used as a marketing tool to persuade people to buy more cigarettes. Popularised by my parents' generation, by the 1950s, the cards had become very collectable. The cards featured sports and famous sportsmen, as well as a host of other subjects, such as plants and animals. Sets usually comprised of 50, sometimes 100. There were thousands in circulation before the Second World War; now they were being brought into schools to be traded and swapped. As well as trading them, you could challenge your friends to a game of 'flicking'. This involved flicking your card from a defined distance towards a wall, while your opponent did the same. The card closest to the wall would win. If you were skilled enough to make the card stand up against the wall, you were a sure winner. I had become very skilled at this game and won hundreds of cards. My favourite set was 'speed' which featured all the speed records on air, land and water. However, somehow all my cards got lost when we moved from Sandwich Stud to Broad Green.

One morning, a new boy came to school whose parents had moved to Beech House Stud. His name was Michael Simms. His parents were Scottish and had moved down from Berwick. Like me, he was a keen footballer, and supported Berwick Rangers, a team of which I had never heard until then. Although Berwick was in Scotland, because it was just across the border from England, the football club played in the English football league. We spent a lot of time together outside of school, including participating in the church choir, the church where we would sometimes attend morning and evening service. When the time came for us to leave school, he decided upon a career in the Royal Navy. I went with him to Cambridge where he attended an initial interview, but I never saw him again after we left school. He did write to me once during his first year as a cadet and enclosed a photograph. He looked splendid in his naval uniform.

Cheveley was a typical village with two pubs – the Star & Garter and The Red Lion – as well as a post office, a bakery and a small Co-op. Any major shopping trips meant catching the bus to Newmarket.

The Co-op stores used to run a type of membership club – the money you spent paid a dividend, so the more you spent the more you got back. Members were given a unique dividend club number so the expenditure could be recorded. Mum's number was 93, easy for us children to remember whenever we were sent to buy groceries. This dividend was important in supporting the household budget, as Mum saved it to spend on clothing and footwear for my brother, sister and I in readiness for starting a new school term. It also helped me get my first pair of football boots with the famous Stanley Matthews signature on the side. Stanley Matthews became a household name after he helped Blackpool win the FA Cup in 1953 against Bolton Wanderers. He was also famous as an England international player.

My dad liked to try his luck on the horses and would have a bet. Mr Matthews, a bookmaker, lived in the village, and most schooldays when I came home for lunch, I was given a slip of paper, upon which was written the name of a horse. As the Matthews' house was a mere 100 yards from the school, it was easy for me to drop off Dad's bet. He very rarely won, despite his in-depth knowledge of horses, especially those he had followed from yearlings to being in training. One day, I decided to change his bet, choosing a horse that had been tipped to win by the Daily Express newspaper. It won, and I got a few shillings. Despite this success, though, I never changed Dad's bet again in case his horse did win!

Mr and Mrs Matthews kept lots of ducks, chickens and geese, so twice a week after school, Jimmy Ranner and I would give them water and collect their eggs, for which we received sixpence. On Sundays, I would walk or cycle to their house to run an additional errand. Mrs Matthews had an elderly mother for whom she cooked Sunday lunch. This, I delivered in a basket to her mother who lived in Church Terrace, a five-minute walk away. For this, I received another sixpence. Sometimes, if the lunch was not ready when I arrived at 1pm, I was given a glass of tonic water while I waited. It was the first time I had tasted this drink; a drink I thought was vile. However, I never refused it as Mum had taught me not refuse an offer of anything, even if you must discard it afterwards.

Though the village had a successful football club, when we first moved there, it did not have a cricket club. The previous cricket team had been disbanded during the war years and hadn't reformed. Cheveley Cricket Club was made famous by Bill Hitch who had played there in the 1880s and who later went on to play county cricket for Surrey and Test cricket for England. In 1955, an inaugural meeting was called to see if there was enough interest to reform the club. There was. Fixtures were initially arranged on Sundays with neighbouring villages. Termed as 'friendlies', they were anything but. At 13, I became a member, initially playing in 20 over evening matches before being selected for the Sunday games. The Sunday games had to end before 6.30pm due to the observance of church evensong services which started at that time. After two years, I was asked if I would take on the role of cricket club secretary. This involved arranging fixtures, both home and away, as well as writing to prominent wealthy people in the village asking them to become vice presidents. Most accepted, considering it an honour to be vice president of the local cricket club, sending money with their acceptance letter.

To earn some pocket money, at 13, I became a newspaper delivery boy. This entailed getting up early before school and cycling to Rolfe's, the village store in the high street, to collect the papers, which had already been sorted in delivery order by Stan Rolfe (who doubled as the newsagent and local baker). The coverage of my first round went from his store, onwards towards the church, then around Church Terrace. This took about half an hour, for which I earned a shilling (5p) a week. Later, I was given a bigger round: down the high street towards the school and then all of Park Road. This was much more lucrative as I got paid half a crown (12.5p) a week. However, it did take much longer, so an earlier start was required, and, even then, it was sometimes a struggle to get them all delivered before school. I very often had to finish the round during the school's lunchbreak after 12.30pm, which did not please some people, as they liked to have their paper to read whilst having breakfast. Once, I fell off my bike, the papers scattered all over the road. As I gathered them up, the order of delivery got mixed up – I had an idea who had what. Though I did my best to deliver them correctly, at the end of the round there were some left over. Being short of time and school beckoning, I threw them over the hedge into the nearest field. I never heard that anyone complained of not having their morning paper that day.

It was also at this time that Mum decided to purchase an evening paper round, delivering the Cambridge Evening News to customers in Cheveley and Saxon Street. Mum was always looking for opportunities to add to the family's income (other than strawberry or apple picking). The profit from each paper was a halfpenny, plus four pence a week for delivery to each household. The number of papers involved was two quires. I never knew before this that a quire was 25 sheets of paper. The papers were delivered by courier to the house at 6pm. This meant that every evening, Monday to Saturday, I would help her do the deliveries after we had had our tea. The deliveries usually took about 2 hours; the round worth just over £4 a week. The paper price was 1.5d. The deliveries were made by bicycle in all weathers, making it quite hard during the winter. Once the final delivery was made on the Saturday evening, we would stop at Auntie Florrie's for a cup of tea and a chat before going home. One of the deliveries was to the Reindeer pub in Saxon Street that ran a pontoon competition using football club names. For one shilling, you were allocated the name of one of the football teams in the English and Scottish leagues. The first team to score 11 goals in one, two, three or more weeks scooped the jackpot. It had to be exactly 11, so if you went over, you continued to the next week. One always hoped for a Scottish team as they were usually the high-scoring teams due to having little competition, as is the case today. I was the winner on one occasion and duly won just over £4. Uncle Will agreed to keep it for me until I really needed it, so I passed it over to him. Several weeks later, I asked him if I could have it back, and he added 10 shillings (50p). I bought an air rifle with the money.

After about a year, my cousin, Neville Godfrey, asked me if I would like to take over his Saturday job as a baker's delivery boy. Stan Rolfe was the baker's delivery man and drove an old, grey van which had seen better days. As well as bread, he carried basic groceries like flour, jam, tinned food and cakes. The round began at 9am from Cheveley village then towards Ashley Road and Newmarket, where supplies of fresh bread were loaded from Dyer's bakery in Wellington Street. Whilst Stan was busy loading the bread, I was given half a crown to get a pound of Musk's famous pork sausages for Stan and his wife's Saturday night tea. Musk's sausages were famous as they had a special recipe and carried the 'by royal appointment' seal above the shop. My next stop was to buy a comic from a paper shop across the road from Dyer's, before then returning. I was always given a bag of cakes by Stan's sister, Constance, who worked at Dyer's. This bag of cakes sustained me for the day as we carried out the bread round.

Starting just outside Newmarket at Ashley Road, we delivered to most properties, including number 38, which would later become a significant address, though I did not know that then. From there, we went to Cheveley village, calling at my house for Mum to select her bread. We usually returned to Rolfe's shop around 1pm. The van would then be reloaded with more bread that had been baked during the morning by 'Wicky', another of Stan's sisters, who made the bread. Stan had four sisters – he was the only male in the Rolfe family. Alongside 'Wicky' and Constance, there was Lol who ran the shop and Cissie who ran the home. None of the sisters were married – only Stan was married, and he lived in Ashley. We had a 30-minute break for lunch, after which we finished the rest of the deliveries in Cheveley village before going on to Saxon Street, Woodditton and Kirtling, returning to Rolfe's store around 6pm. For this, I earned seven shillings and six pence (35.5p). Once paid, I would go into the shop and purchase a box of Bassett's Liquorice Allsorts, as they were Mum's favourite, and give them to her when I arrived home. I enjoyed the experience of the bread round, meeting many different families and characters.

A loaf of bread cost seven and a half pence (3p), eight pence if it was a cut loaf. I got to know the distinct types of bread and loaf shapes, such as sandwich, cottage, tin, cob, white twist, and milk loaf. If there was a major sporting event on a Saturday, such as the Grand National or FA Cup Final, Stan would always make sure we arrived at a house with a TV in order that we could spend a bit of time watching the event. I still remember watching the 1956 FA Cup Final between Birmingham City and Manchester City, the match when Manchester City goalkeeper, Bert Trautmann, played with a broken neck!

A year later, I added to my Saturday assistant baker's round, taking on a job previously done by my cousin, Neville. After Neville finished school and no longer wanted the work, Stan asked me to take over three evenings a week from 4–6pm, Mondays, Wednesdays and Fridays. For this, I earned an extra shilling (5p) each day. The evening round went from the high street through the village, concluding at Broad Green.

One summer morning in my last year at Cheveley CofE School, Constance Rolfe came into the school to speak to Mr Moore. I was asked to step out into the passageway, where I learned that Stan had been involved in a serious accident whilst travelling down Ashley Road to Newmarket to load up at Dyer's bakery. He had been taken to Newmarket General Hospital. Constance asked Mr Moore if I could be excused from school for a couple of days to show her the bread round, as she now had to step in and deliver the bread to the villages. Mr Moore said if my parents agreed, then that would be fine. It was a tough call for my parents to make as I was studying for my exam to attend Cambridge Technical College that September. However, I felt that I could manage the request. Besides, without my knowledge of all the customers' requirements and addresses, the bread could not be supplied. Consequently, Rolfe's could lose its customers if they had to find an alternative bakery.

Constance owned a black saloon car which we loaded with bread on cloths laid all over the back seats. We then set off. Knowing the route, I directed her to each address, and together we supplied the bread for each family over the next two days. It was then Saturday, when I would be on the round again. The following week, she felt she knew the round well enough to be able to remember all the customers' addresses and bread requirements. Stan was in hospital for several weeks, but he did recover and was able to resume the deliveries. Constance then returned to working in Dyer's bakery shop. When I left school at the end of the summer term, 1958, in the September my brother, Dennis, took over my baker's delivery job.

Another job I took over from my cousin Neville was as bellringer and clock winder at Cheveley Parish Church. For this, I was paid 10 shillings a month (50p). The job involved ringing the church bells on a Sunday before morning and evening services and winding up the church clock twice a week. To do this, I used a key to unlock the door that led up to the belfry, but because the key was large and heavy, it was kept behind a drainpipe near the door. Once the door was opened, stone steps led up to the first floor where the bellringing ropes and the clock mechanism were. The steps continued to the second floor where five bells in various sizes were slung on a framework of large beams. The steps then continued further up to a small door that opened out to the roof. From the lead-covered roof, you had a view across the whole village.

Every Sunday, I rang the bells 15 minutes before each morning and evening service to remind people of the day and time. My cousin taught me the sequence of pulling the bell ropes, which came down from the actual bells onto a wooden frame so that one person could ring them. The sequence was: one, two, three, one, two, four, three, two, four, five. This was repeated until five minutes before the service began, when only number five bell would be rung every second. I was never very musical, but mastered the bellringing, and during practice evenings would learn to play 'Now the Day is Over' and some other hymns. On occasion, when a wedding was taking place, there was also a request for the bells to be rung as the bride and bridegroom came out of the church. For this, I was paid extra. The other time the bells had to be rung was one second after midnight on 31 December to welcome in the New Year.

The winding of the clock had to be done twice during the week, as well as on Sundays. This involved winding up the quarter-bell chime and the hour-bell chime. Both had large weights that had to be rewound. This was done by inserting a large handle into the mechanism and hauling it round and round until the weights were back at the top. The quarter-chime weight was not too bad, but the hour one was a struggle as it was heavy. In September 2021, I returned by invitation to the belfry after 63 years. The clock had since been converted to the World Clock and was controlled electronically by satellite signal (no more winding by hand). It was a nostalgic moment climbing the steps into the belfry after all those years, and my host, Ceilia, allowed me to ring the bells once again. Despite the passing years, I could still ring out the sequence, and had my photo taken!

I enjoyed the last two years at school – from both an academic point of view and because of the sporting activities. Though the school did not have many competitive fixtures as far as football and cricket were concerned, Mr Moore did take a lot of interest in my selection for the Cheveley cricket team and football club. (His son, Alan, was also a team member who no doubt relayed my performances to his father.) During the summer of 1958, I took the examination to attend Cambridge Technical College of Art. This was open to pupils who had failed their eleven-plus exam for entrance to grammar school. This time I was successful and felt quite sad at the thought of leaving Cheveley CofE School, where I had spent six enjoyable, and eventful, years.

3

LANE'S FARM, MOULTON

During the summer school holidays of 1958, I asked Dad if there was any work at the Sandwich Stud that I could do until I went to Cambridge in September. I had previously driven the stud's grey Ferguson tractor, voluntarily, when the men were collecting hay, so I thought that there was a possibility of doing that again. Dad, however, did not think there was. Instead, he suggested Lane's Farm, in the nearby village of Moulton, would be a better option. One evening, after tea, we both cycled down to the farm, but it appeared deserted. This was because the farm manager and workers were several fields away bringing in the corn harvest.

We located the correct field by the noise of the combine harvester – a Massey-Harris – and cycled over. The farm manager, Mr Morley, was engaged in a discussion with his foreman, so Dad waited until he had finished before approaching him. He asked if there was any work I could be given whilst on holiday from school, motioning towards me. Mr Morley, who had a dark complexion and bushy eyebrows, looked towards me as though weighing up my physique. He said:

"Come along tomorrow morning at 8 o'clock and we'll see what we can do."

I was absolutely thrilled.

I arrived the next morning having cycled from home, which took about 15 minutes, and reported to the farmyard where all the other workers were gathered, awaiting the farm's foreman, Bob Millar, to issue the daily tasks. I was to wait for Mr Morley. He soon appeared and set me the task of gathering plums from the manor house garden! I was a bit disappointed as I was looking forward to helping in the harvest fields, but the upside was, whatever task I was given, I would be earning money. The plum picking took almost two days as it involved climbing amongst the branches of the trees while avoiding the wasps! I reflected later that this is what Mr Morley was sizing me up for when Dad asked if I could have a job. At the age of 15, I had not been subjected to much physical work, so was flat-chested and without much muscle power.

Once the plum picking was over, I was shown how to topple over the corn stooks that had been standing in rows in the field so that they would dry out following some rain the previous week. This was necessary so that they could be collected and stacked for winter. I was joined by two other workers who appeared close to retiring; one of them, bent almost double, was called Walter. Walter drove a car that resembled a bubble as it had a glass dome capsule over a motorbike engine. It was in fact his invalid car.

Lane's Farm comprised several hundred acres and extended right up to the boundary on the west to Sandwich Stud, and Dalham Hall Stud to the east. Most of the land was arable farming with fields of wheat, barley and oats. There was also some land set aside for sugar beet. Although the farm had a modern combine harvester, most of the fields of wheat, oat and barley were cut by tractor and binder. This machine cut the straw of the corn and bundled it into sheaves and then tied the sheaf with string before ejecting it out to land on the field. The farmworkers then collected each sheaf, one under each arm, and stood them up with the ears of corn at the top pointing towards each other, the straw base of the sheaf angled to the ground. This was to help the ears of corn to ripen before they were collected for storing. Six to eight of these were placed together to form stooks. I became part of the team doing this task, which was very rough on bare arms, an occasional prickly thistle trussed up with the straw.

The farm employed eight or so permanent workers who I got on with very well, especially when it came to collecting the sheaves. Each person took turns driving the tractor whilst the others either pitched the sheaves up or loaded them onto the trailer. There was a technique to pitching up – it had to be presented to the loader with the bottom facing out. The loader had to work quickly as sheaves were constantly being pitched up, so the load gradually got higher until a halt was called when it was considered high enough. Another trailer would then pull alongside, and the loader would slide down into it to start the process again for another load. Meanwhile, the full load would be taken to a Dutch barn (a barn with just a roof), where it would be unloaded by another team and stored until threshing time, usually in February and March. The purpose of storing the sheaves over the winter this way was to even out the supply of grain to the market, where, in the later months, a better price could be obtained.

I really enjoyed the outdoor life, and the physical work helped me to put on some muscle, particularly in my upper body. The other bonus was that I was earning around five pounds including overtime, for a week's work. When it was too damp for the harvest work, usually in the morning, I was given the job of cutting the lawns of the manor house with a petrol mower and weeding a field of mangles (a type of turnip fed to animals in the winter) by hand. I hated this laborious job of pulling up the weeds that had grown in between the rows of mangles. This weed was known as 'fat hen' and was as tall as me in places, so working along the row, I soon accumulated an armful. The field was in earshot of the church clock which chimed every quarter hour. How slow time seemed to go. I was pleased when it eventually chimed five o clock, so I could leave.

It had been a wonderful sweltering summer, and, as the final harvest was being gathered in the first week of September 1958, thunder was heard in the distance and lightning flashes could be seen on the horizon. The lightning appeared normal at first but then turned to brilliant reds, blues and greens, which seemed to go on for an exceptionally long time, accompanied by the occasional clap of thunder. Eric Tweed, one of the farmworkers, said he had not seen lightning like it since he was in the army serving in India. The final load of sheaves had safely been gathered in, and I had got home before the storm arrived. My mum, who always removed all cutlery from the table and turned around mirrors in case of a lightning strike, had already taken these precautions as I walked in. Within half an hour, the storm erupted in full fury, very heavy rain and thunder that went on for several hours before petering out, only to return a few hours later during the night.

The following week, I said goodbye to everyone at the farm, received my last pay packet, and prepared myself for college in Cambridge.

After finishing college in Cambridge in mid-July 1959, I decided to go back to Lane's Farm for the harvest period and then evaluate my future. By this time, I had a Norman Nippy, a 50cc moped that my mum had bought me. So instead of cycling, I used the moped to get to Lane's Farm. This 'bicycle with an engine' (as the older farmworkers called it) created much interest, but it saved me pedalling back home each day up a steep hill. By the time I started back at the farm, the harvest period had begun, and I was once again in the thick of it – stooking, pitching, and loading the sheaves. This time, I was there long enough to help gather the straw bales which were heavier than the sheaves of corn. So, to pitch these you needed a person at each side. Being left-handed, I was in great demand, whilst most of the others, being right-handed, had to reverse their grip if they were paired with someone who was also right-handed.

Life at the farm got more varied when the harvest was over, as the fields were cultivated and ploughed, with all the debris and old straw that had not been baled having to be cleared. Every Thursday after 10 October, I accompanied Mr Morley, Pat Jennings, a neighbouring farmer, and Jodie Green, the landlord of The King's Head, Moulton, on a shooting trip. My job was to help flush out pheasants and other game for these men, who carried 12-bore shotguns. I then shouldered the bag used for carrying the kill. We covered several miles during these afternoons, as did the two spaniel dogs that belonged to Mr Green. I had never seen gundogs in action; they were amazing at picking up the birds that had been taken down and bringing them to me, with their incredibly soft mouths, to be placed in the game bag. Some days, I got very wet, especially if it had been raining and we were walking through the field of sugar beet, beating the leaves to drive out the birds. Pat Jennings was the best shot and seemed to bag more than the others, but they shared the spoils between them – pheasant, hares, partridge, and rabbit. On one occasion, Jennings managed to shoot a woodcock, an amazingly fast bird no bigger than mistle thrush. I learned that this was the ultimate prize as, due to their speed, they were difficult to shoot.

As autumn approached, I was set the job of gathering apples from the apple orchard and taking them to the apple store. Here, they were examined for bruises. The unblemished fruit was wrapped in newspaper, then placed on shelves in an old storehouse. The orchard was big, so this job, day after day, became very boring; the job I continued doing until the sugar beet was ready to be harvested. This involved a tractor with a machine that went between two rows and lifted them so that they formed a single row. The job for the workers, of which I was one, was to cut the tops off with a beet hook and make piles ready for collecting. The beet hook was a very sharp tool, more like a machete with a hook on the end, which you used to pick the whole beet before grabbing the root with one hand and chopping off the top. It was a dangerous job as you could easily slice off a finger, especially on a frosty morning when you could hardly feel your hands.

The piles of topped beet were then thrown on a trailer with a special beet fork that had rounded tines instead of points, so you did not pierce the beet. They were then dumped at the side of the field where they would later be collected and taken to the sugar beet factory in Bury St. Edmunds and turned into sugar or molasses.

Once the sugar beet had been harvested, there was little work on the land to be done and I thought I might be asked to leave, but Mr Morley was happy for me to continue, viewing me as he did as a future, permanent, young employee. Most of the others were much older, apart from Bob Newall, with whom I became very friendly. Bob was in his mid-30s and had a young family, and, like all the workers, lived in a tied cottage. This was very much a feature and expectation of employed farmworkers. They earned a much-reduced wage but were compensated by living in a property owned by the farm, paying a token rent of just a few shillings. This was why many of the workers at the farm were getting on, as, if they left, they would need to find another home. It was also how the farm retained the workers' loyalty. Very feudal.

As autumn moved into winter, we were sent out in teams, hedging and coppicing around the fields. This was an important winter job so that the hedges were kept cut back and headlands cleared. One had to learn to use a slasher, which was a long-handled sharp blade, like a grass hook, that slashed at the hedge and grass. Shaping the hedge was important and tall hedges had to be cut and layered, a technique that needed a lot of skill, as demonstrated by the older workers. The weather was mostly frosty in the mornings, so the debris we cut down was used to start a fire which was useful to sit around during tea breaks and lunchtime.

The highlight of the day, if you were working alongside the main road between Moulton and Gazeley, was when the girls working in Newmarket would cycle by in the morning, and again, late in the afternoon. There was one girl I found attractive, so one day I plucked up enough courage to ask her out. I caught her up on my moped and she agreed that I could meet her one evening in the village, telling me where to be at a certain time. She lived in Ousden. I duly arrived after my tea, and, in the dark, found the wooden bridge she had mentioned that crossed over a small brook, and waited. I did not think she was going to turn up at first and was about to go home, when she appeared. Her name was Heather Smith, aged 18. We spent a couple of hours talking, though I can't remember about what, before arranging to meet again the following week. We met up at the same place three more times; the last time we walked together on the road out towards Wickhambrook. It was a windy night, so, seeing a barn, we sat inside and talked some more then walked back. We arranged to meet again the following week, but she did not turn up. I do not even recall us kissing as I was shy. Maybe she wanted someone who was a bit more forthcoming.

Christmas and New Year came and went, and I was still working at Lane's Farm, hedging, keeping pathways through the woods clear, and being the shooting assistant on Thursdays. Thoughts occasionally turned to a different type of job, but I loved the outdoors, and on Sundays would meet up with Bob Newall to go for a Sunday pint at the pub in Ousden and a game of darts, at which I had become quite good.

In mid-February, the nature of the work on the farm changed – it was time to thresh out the sheaves that had been stored since the end of the harvest. Churchman's, the agricultural contractors, turned up with all the farm machinery needed for this purpose. As well as the threshing machine, they had elevators and a baling machine for the straw. I was made 'chaff' boy, which involved taking the bags of chaff off the threshing machine and emptying them in a big pile. I thought this was a nice, easy job as the bags of chaff were noticeably light. However, I did not expect it to be so dusty – chaff flew about everywhere, especially when taking off one bag and putting on another. There were two places for the bags to be fixed where the chaff came out, so, as one was being emptied, the other one filled up. It was demanding work trying to keep up, the bags filling very quickly. Failure to keep it clear would block the machine, so I couldn't afford to slow down.

It was in early March when my parents received an unexpected visit from Bill Challis and his son, Mick, who ran W.A. Challis Agricultural Contractors. They knocked on the door and asked my mum if they could speak to me. Knowing that I had some experience at Lane's Farm, they wanted to employ me as a tractor driver. They had recently taken on more work and needed another person to fulfil the extra contracts. I decided immediately to take the job, and the next day I went to see Mr Morley to give a week's notice, which I found quite hard to do. He wished me good luck. A week later, I said goodbye to everyone for the last time, all except Bob Newall. For some time afterwards, he and I continued to meet up on a Sunday for a pint and a game of darts.

4

CAMBRIDGE

In the first week of September 1958, I was on a steam train from Newmarket to Cambridge. I had taken, and passed, what was known as the Arts and Craft exam in my last term at Cheveley CofE Junior School. Passing the exam meant I had gained a place at the Cambridge School of Art and Technology.

The subject was an FPB course – Full-Time Building Preliminary. It was a year's course in which I learned all about the trades connected with building, such as plumbing, carpentry and joinery, plastering, bricklaying, architecture, technical drawing, and painting and decorating. There were 16 of us on the course from all over Cambridgeshire. We stayed as one group for the technical lectures but were split into two groups for the practical work. The purpose of the course was to provide us with some experience of the different trades, so, at the end of the year, we would choose one as a preferred career.

Each morning, I had to cycle three-and-a-half miles from my home at Sandwich Stud to Newmarket Station to catch the train. I usually met up with Pauline Mayes at Broomstick Corner, Cheveley, where she had cycled in from her home in the neighbouring village of Ashley. She was also attending the college, doing a secretarial course. I knew Pauline as she had been a pupil at Cheveley school, though had left a year earlier than me, she now in her second year at what was termed

'The Tech'. It was good to meet up each morning and cycle together, as whilst there was no relationship as such, we did have a lot in common, having both attended the same school. When we arrived at the station, we had an arrangement whereby instead of leaving our bicycles there, we parked them at the home of Miss Nevard, our former teacher from Cheveley CofE Junior School whose house was next to the station.

Pauline had made friends in her first year with two other girls on the same course as her. They met up at the station each morning, and I also became part of the group. Their names were Cynthia Rose and Susan Frostick, and each morning as the train arrived, if it was vacant, we made sure we all sat together in the first carriage immediately behind the engine.

Upon our arrival at the station in Cambridge, it was then a 25-minute walk to the college in Mill Road. There, we split up to go to our different departments. At the end of the day, providing our lecture times were similar, we would meet up again to walk to the station and catch the train back to Newmarket. I do not know how it came about, but somehow, I always carried Cynthia's case, with her books in, as well as my own.

In my first morning in class, there was a roll call, and my name was called out first. Usually, names are called in alphabetical order, but not so this time. I do not know what this signified. Had I been top of the entrance exam, or the bottom? I never found out. I ended up seated at the front, next to a boy called Edward Barton. He was from Newmarket, and his father had a greengrocer's shop on what was known as the Rookery in the middle of town and a stall in the high street on market days.

The year was very intense, not only with the practical side for carpentry, bricklaying, plumbing, plastering, painting, and architecture, but also the theory for each of these subjects. Other academic subjects included maths, geography, algebra, technical drawing and physics. I found physics fascinating but quite hard as it was a subject I had not studied at Cheveley. I was also at a disadvantage with the laboratory experiments which were new to me, whereas the other boys had either done them before or already had a basic knowledge. To break up the week, we also had subjects like current affairs, even music. My interest in music was never great, and the opportunity was missed as I found learning about composers and how to read music was not as important as watching one of the county's cricket teams playing the University of Cambridge at the famous Fenners ground, only five minutes away. A few of us interested in cricket would miss the music class and climb over the wall to watch the teams practising mid-morning before play began. I remember seeing the Surrey side of that time which included the Bedser twins, Alec and Eric, as well as Tony Lock and Jim Laker, the famous 'spin twins' who played Test cricket for England. Jim Laker still holds the Test record of taking 19 wickets for 90 runs against Australia in 1956 at Old Trafford, Manchester.

Outdoor walkabout lessons were also arranged to visit buildings in Cambridge to appreciate the architecture: the Round Church and Fitzwilliam Museum were particularly interesting.

Lunch breaks were spent lazing around on Parker's Piece, a communal park area in the centre of Cambridge, or playing football until it was time for the afternoon lectures. At that time, on the opposite side of Parker's Piece, a large construction was being built. My cousin, Derek Hicks, was working there, so the football kickabout was often against the construction workers. The construction turned out to be an indoor swimming pool, where, 10 years later, I attended adult learn-to-swim classes and learnt breaststroke with colleagues from Sprites.

At the end of July 1959, the course concluded with exams. I finished in eighth place. I still had no idea what career I was going to choose, but had always enjoyed technical drawing, so I was given two interviews with firms for the position of apprentice draughtsman. One was with Chivers, a firm located in Histon, famous for making jam, and the other was with a Cambridge firm called Carter Jonas. I was not successful with either. Though I ended my year at Cambridge Tech without a job, I now had a good basic knowledge of the various building trades.

Fellow classmate Edward Barton started an apprenticeship as a bricklayer with a Newmarket building firm called Holland's. I met him in Newmarket soon after we had left Cambridge, and he informed me that the firm were also looking for apprentice carpenters. I decided to apply and wrote to them, but when I got a reply, they informed me that the vacancies had already been filled.

By the time the college year ended, daily travel by steam train had also changed; steam-powered locomotives were being replaced by trains powered by diesel. Looking back on that year, it was a pivotal point: I grew up and met new friends; it was the first time I had been to another school since we moved to Cheveley. The girls I travelled with regularly were a source of fun and whilst no serious relationship existed, I did eventually go out with Pauline a few times to the pictures in Newmarket after I had left college. Cynthia also got to know my cousin, Neville Godfrey, so we would occasionally make up a foursome, and even went on a daytrip to Cambridge using our college rail passes where we had a picnic by the River Cam. I did keep in touch with Pauline for about a year afterwards, and Cynthia as well, as she was going out with Neville. However, once he was called up for national service, I lost contact with her. She did, however, try to look me up when she visited Scotland sometime in the 1990s, but I was away at a company conference and missed her.

As for Pauline, we rekindled our friendship after her husband died, and Kate, my wife, had also died. I now stay with Pauline whenever I am visiting Newmarket, which is at least once a year, to catch up with my brother, sister, and other friends. Pauline also likes to come up to Scotland for a visit and stays with me. We both appreciate each other's company, being on our own as we are for most of the time.

In August 1959, rather than laze about and do nothing, I decided to return to Lane's Farm at Moulton to help with the harvesting, like I had done the previous year. I also needed to start earning my own money as my parents had supported me during my time at Cambridge. Little did I know that I would stay at the farm until March 1960.

5

W.A. CHALLIS
AGRICULTURAL CONTRACTORS

I had known of W.A. Challis since my schooldays, as they were a firm of agricultural contractors that harvested most of the cornfields around the villages of Cheveley and the Newmarket area. Originally, they had done the work with a tractor and binder, but, more recently, used a combine harvester. Before the outbreak of myxomatosis, a disease rabbits contracted, rabbit was a popular dish for dinner. So, as youngsters, we used to follow the combine harvester from field to field, ready to flush out the rabbits as soon as the corn was cut down. When I was a schoolboy, driving a combine harvester had had a certain attraction; now here I was, working for this agricultural firm, being given an opportunity to do just that.

On my first morning, I arrived at the 'yard' (as it was known) in Ashley village, where all the tractors and machinery were kept, and was introduced to Henry Benton, the senior tractor driver, and John Harris, the only other employee. A few years later, John became my brother-in-law when he married my sister.

Mick Challis, the only son of Bill Challis, delegated the work each day, and, on my first morning, I was told to go with John Harris to Side Hill Stud. The job was to spread 'basic slag' over the stud's paddocks. This entailed loading a spreader onto a low loader in the yard and then travelling down to Side Hill Stud, which was located just outside

Newmarket. Two tractors were needed: one to take the spreader and the other to pull the spreader across the paddock. John, having worked for the company for just over a year, drove a Ford Major, attached to which was the low loader, while I drove a grey Ferguson TE20. Thousands of Ferguson TE20s were manufactured between 1946–1956, becoming a popular post-Second World War farm tractor. This model ran on TVO – tractor vaporising oil – (or paraffin, as it was more commonly known). The tractor had to be started on petrol, and then, once warmed up, switched over to paraffin.

Upon arrival at Side Hill Stud, we met Dick Cole, the farm manager, who showed us which paddocks needed spreading. Bernard Van Cutsem, a famous racehorse owner, owned Side Hill Stud. He believed that 'basic slag' spread on the paddocks would produce lush grass feed, beneficial to his racehorses. I had never heard of this material, which came in 56lb bags and was nothing more than black powder. The material is produced through the open-hearth method of steelmaking and is used to amend highly acidic soil, like that of ground limestone. The work turned out to be a very dusty job, especially when turning into the breeze (this was before the days of tractor cabs, so we were constantly exposed to the elements). John and I took turns on the spreader – one of us loading the spreader and the other doing the actual spreading. By the end of the day, we had completed the paddocks and returned home. My new blue boilersuit, the tractor driver's uniform, was black with dust, so I had to take it off before being allowed inside the house.

The next day, I was to join Mick Challis, who would be planting the spring barley on the farm of Mr Sadler, a well-known Cheveley farmer. This job entailed using a seed drill pulled by a tractor that was loaded with barley seed and fertiliser. My job was to stand on the back of the drill and make sure the individual drill pipes did not get blocked. If they did, there would be gaps when the seeds grew. Mick drove the tractor as I was not yet experienced enough to do so. When we reached the end of the headland, my next role was to kick the chain over that pulled the harrow behind, so that the harrow covered in the seed, leaving a line as a marker for the next lap. There was no safety rail to prevent me falling off the back and getting caught up in the harrows, so holding onto a grabrail and keeping my balance was essential. I spent the rest of the week with Mick Challis, doing this until all the fields were sown. It was not an easy task standing on the drill. It was also quite physical, having to reload the drill with sacks of barley seed and fertilizer. I was pleased that I had become used to the physical work at Lane's Farm and acquired the strength and fitness needed now.

The following week, I was back on my Ferguson tractor, chain harrowing the paddocks at Wyck Hall Stud. This process entailed pulling a chain harrow over the paddocks to remove the dead grass (thatch) which had accumulated over the winter, allowing fresh growth to come through.

In November 1960, Bill Challis died after a short illness. His son, Mick, became the boss, assisted by his mother, who managed the invoices, wages and timesheets. As Mick was now responsible for getting the work and negotiating contracts, he became less involved in the day-to-day work. This meant I was given more responsibility working on my own. I enjoyed the variety of work, as each day I never knew where I would be going or what job was needed.

W.A. Challis had contracts with most of the stud farms in Cheveley and Newmarket, as well as the racehorse training establishments, so it was great meeting new people. Being involved in the complete farming cycle was an experience – ploughing, sowing, harvesting, then ploughing again. In between, during May and June, came the haymaking season. This was when we cut all the grass in the paddocks of the stud farms that had let their grass grow long. This grass was then turned until it was dried by the sun, transforming it into hay. Once dry enough, it was gathered into oblong bales, then collected and stored undercover for use as animal feed in the winter. I still believe to this day that I became immune to hay fever from having to endure the pollen that drifted up from the grass in the air as the machine cut it down. Baling hay was my favourite job: seeing the dried grass picked up and rammed into an oblong shape, tied automatically by the baling machine, then ejected from the baler. It would be collected later by the stud or farm staff and stored, before it could be spoilt by the weather.

Mick was more forward-looking than his father had been, and, in the summer of 1961, he purchased two, second-hand Massey Ferguson combine harvesters with a 12ft cutter bar, complete with grain silos. This was a considerable investment, as previously there had only been an 8ft Massey-Harris that required the grain to be bagged by hand. John and I were each allocated one to drive; Henry preferred the CLAAS combine which had to be pulled by a Nuffield tractor. With the new machinery, now more work could be undertaken during the harvesting season.

As summer moved into autumn, Mick Challis decided to invest in a sugar beet harvester. I was given the responsibility of learning about this new machine and how to operate it. Using a machine to harvest sugar beet had become fashionable – previously it was a very labour-intensive job, done by hand. Now, the machine did the job four times faster, cutting off the tops, lifting the beet, and transporting them up into a trailer that ran alongside. The driver towing the trailer had to be very alert and keep pace with me driving the harvester. If he was too far in front, the beet would fall to the ground, if he was too far behind, he'd get hit on the head!

Other than ploughing in readiness for the spring, the agricultural business slowed down during the winter months. To keep the three of us busy, Mick had contracts with the local Cambridgeshire council to grit the roads. This we did early in the morning after frost had made them slippery, and, when the snow fell, we were tasked with using the snowplough to keep them clear. I was on call for the Cheveley area, and, if the weather was bad, would receive a knock on the door by Bill

Davey, the council foreman, around 6am. I then had to get up and take out the tractor and trailer, which were stored at Mick's house, load the trailer with grit with the help of Bill and another worker, and then drive slowly down the middle of each road whilst they manually distributed the grit using shovels. (There were no automatic spreading machines in the 1960s!) If a vehicle appeared, it meant pulling over to one side and letting it pass. On occasion, after a late night out, I was too tired to be woken early, so the council foreman gave up and called Mick Challis, who would take over until I arrived.

The winter of 1962/3 proved to be the longest on record and was certainly the coldest I can remember. It started snowing on Boxing Day and the freeze lasted until early March. Many homes became cut off from water supplies as the frost penetrated the ground and froze the water in the old cast iron pipes. As a result, all homes built today are connected to a frostproof polyurethane pipe.

Ploughing and sowing became late, due to the severity of the winter, as the only work other than the gritting was spreading manure on the fields. This entailed clearing out cattle sheds with a tractor, to which a forklift was attached. The manure was loaded onto spreaders and then spread over the fields. It was dirty, smelly work, but at least we were gainfully employed.

One evening in early March, the council workers and I were busy loading the trailer with grit, preparing to grit the roads again, when we became aware of the sound of water dripping. The trees were thawing, and water was falling from them. We immediately stopped loading grit and headed back home; the big thaw had at last started. This resulted in many burst waterpipes and flooding, but thankfully we weren't affected at home.

Despite the late sowing that year, the harvest did not suffer, and the season continued as before. The winter of 1964 was milder than the previous one, so it was business as usual for the farming and stud community.

Though I loved this outdoor life and the variety of work, I knew that one day it had to end as the pay was not particularly good. By now, Kate and I were married – 6th June 1964, 20 years after D-Day. We had saved a deposit for a new house in Newmarket and moved in in September. Our next-door neighbour, Les Hockley, a former police sergeant, was the personnel manager at Sprite Caravans. It was while I was busy seeding a new front lawn in October, that he asked me if I would be interested in a job. Sprite Caravans were recruiting new operatives to work on the production line. The pay was £17 a week for a Grade 'C' starter, double what I was earning at W.A Challis. He said all I needed was a hammer, hacksaw and pincers. I discussed this with Kate, and we decided that it was time to make a fresh start. I agreed to start the following week – after I had given in my notice to W.A. Challis.

As I'd been harvesting sugar beet in the village of Isleham for Mr Turner, a local farmer, I had not had the opportunity to give in my notice. Usually, Mick Challis would call during the week to see how I was progressing but had not been out to see me. So, on the Friday evening, I went to his house to say that I wanted to give a week's notice. He had been particularly good to me, so I found this difficult and began by saying that I wished I had come on more pleasant terms. I then explained that I wanted to give notice as I had been offered a job at Sprites. He knew the reason: more money.

"I shall be sorry to lose you," he said. "But even if I offered you a pay rise, I cannot compete with what you will earn at Sprites. I can see your mind is made up."

A week later, the last Friday in October 1964, I parked the tractor and harvester on the headland, climbed down from the farm vehicle, and drove home to Kate.

My time as an agricultural contract tractor and combine driver had ended. I felt quite sad, but I was now a married man and knew it was time to move on.

6

CATHERINE BAKER

A friend's 21st birthday party on 23 July 1960, was to have an impact on me for the rest of my life. For it was here that I met 18-year-old Catherine Baker, known as Kate. The party was hosted by the parents of my friend, Geoff Gammon, the venue a marquee erected on the front lawn of their Chevelely bungalow. As a friend of their son, I was invited, along with most of the other Cheveley teenage boys, a group of us who went around together and played football and cricket for the village teams.

Geoff was his parents' only child. His father was the local milkman and his mother was lovely, a housewife of that time, always very welcoming. She would give us lemonade and sweets whenever we visited. Two years previously, in September 1958, I had been on holiday to Manchester with Geoff. He had relatives there and was thinking of applying for a place at Manchester University to study chemistry, so he invited me along to check out the area. I particularly remember the holiday, as it was only six months after the Munich air disaster in which most of the Manchester United football team, known as the Busby Babes, were killed. The team had had to be rebuilt with ageing stars, plus one or two who had survived the crash, including Bobby Charlton. During our holiday, Geoff and I went to Old Trafford to watch them play an evening match against Sheffield Wednesday.

We also saw Stockport County play, in those days, a Football League Division 3 team.

The trip to Manchester was the first time I had been away on holiday without my parents, so it was extremely exciting, being in such a big city as Manchester. Notable events were going to the cinema to see The Ten Commandments being shown in CinemaScope for the first time, and Manchester experiencing a drought – some mornings, no water came out of the tap!

Geoff's birthday party was held on the Saturday evening in the marquee with some soft drinks and beer. There was music from a record player, and everyone was having an enjoyable time. Kate had come with Pauline Southgate, her best friend, who had been going out with Geoff at the time. The two of them were busy socialising that night. There were other girls there, but I noticed Kate as she was enjoying the party. To my disappointment, she sat on the knee of one of my other friends, Alan Moore, the son of my former headmaster. However, a couple of dances later, I was rewarded when she came and sat on my knee, and we were able to have a chat. I was immediately attracted to her. We seemed to get along quite well; so much so, I suggested we went for a short walk. She agreed. We didn't go far – we stood in a neighbour's drive a few paces down the road and chatted some more before we kissed. The neighbour's gate had the name St. Catherine's written on it, and Kate said, "Look, that's my name." We chatted a bit more and kissed again.

Before returning to the party, she said, "Can I see you tomorrow?"

"Yes, but you will have to come to a cricket match. Cheveley Cricket Club is playing a cup semi-final tomorrow at Longstanton, just outside Cambridge. I am in the team, as is Geoff and some of the other boys at the party. We are all travelling in the team coach, so we can stop and collect you on the way."

Though I hadn't had a regular girlfriend before, I had dated one or two girls. I was not expecting Kate to come to the cricket, but, sure enough, she was waiting with Pauline to be picked up the next day.

The cricket match was a success. We progressed through to the final, thanks to a great performance of left-arm bowling by Alan Moore. I do not remember the scores, but these can be found in the old scorebooks of Cheveley Cricket Club.

For the next few weeks, Kate and I saw each other a lot, either going to the pictures at one of the Newmarket cinemas or meeting with friends for a drink at The Red Lion pub in Cheveley. This pub was the social gathering place for us Cheveley teenagers, and was run by Eric and May Mayell, a great couple, who had allowed me to play for the darts team when aged only 15. In those days, the girls would drink Babycham or Cherry B, whilst the boys' drink was usually a pint of brown and mild: a half-pint of mild beer from the barrel mixed with a half-pint of Greene King Burton's bottled brown ale.

Kate worked as a dispensing assistant for Boots the chemists in Newmarket, her first job after leaving Ely High School for Girls. She would cycle to Cheveley in the evening after work to meet me and then we would cycle together to The Red Lion. After a couple of drinks and an evening of socialising, I would take her home via the Cheveley recreation ground, where we would stop off for a kiss and a cuddle. When going to the pictures, I would either cycle or ride my moped to her house – 38 Ashley Road, Newmarket. One Sunday after lunch, I cycled over as usual, having arranged to meet her. However, I was met by Pauline on her bike, looking sad. She handed me a letter from Kate. Kate had written to say how sorry she was, but she wanted to call off our courtship. Pauline waited whilst I read the letter, and, knowing the content, said, "I'm sorry, Mick."

I was surprised and could not understand what had gone wrong. "Go back and tell her that I've not read the letter, and I need to see her. I'll wait."

About half an hour passed before Kate appeared, cycling towards me. As she reached me, she was visibly upset, crying into a big white handkerchief. She said, "I'm really sorry."

I put my arm around her, and said, "Let us talk about it."

We sat on the field of Side Hill Stud where she told me she had been to a dance on the Saturday in Newmarket and had enjoyed the company of another boy, who had worn an attractive red sweater. She had agreed to see him again. I was not prepared to give up that easily; I really enjoyed being with Kate and was beginning to fall in love with her. We discussed the situation for a couple of hours and agreed to continue seeing each other.

Our relationship went from strength to strength after that episode; so much so, we would see each other every evening after work. Eventually, Kate was introduced to my parents. Mum and Dad really liked her and were pleased that I now had a steady girlfriend instead of spending time in the local pub with my male friends. I was also invited to meet Kate's parents, who made me very welcome, as did her grandparents who lived in the same bungalow.

Kate and Pauline would support me and Geoff at cricket matches and were watching when Cheveley won the Jack Branch Cup Final at Teversham, defeating Great Shelford. The club celebrated by holding a dinner at the White Lion Hotel in Newmarket and Kate came as my partner. Attending this formal dinner together was a memorable occasion for us both.

Kate was very musical, having attained grade eight piano at the age of only 14. She was also keen on dancing. So, I enrolled at the Simpson School of Dance held at the Carlton ballroom in Newmarket. After many lessons in ballroom, jive, and some Latin, I entered and passed the exam in waltz, foxtrot and quickstep, gaining a bronze medal, which Kate already had. We developed our own jive routine and would attend the dances at the Carlton ballroom on a Saturday night, rock & roll by now in full swing. Every month, well-known musicians like Joe Brown, Gerry and the Pacemakers, and many more would play at the Memorial Hall in Newmarket and Kate and I would go along. Once a month, a trip to Cambridge was arranged to see rising stars in the pop world. On one occasion, Helen Shapiro was the star billing and The Beatles a support group. If only we knew then the success they would later have as they sat drinking coffee in the same café as us after a show!

Kate was also exceptionally good at singing and had a lovely soprano voice. Every Thursday afternoon, which was her half-day off work, she would have advanced singing lessons in Cambridge. As a member of NOMADS (Newmarket Operatic Musical and Dramatic Society), she was active in regular amateur dramatics. We would support each other, she with my sport and me with her music and drama.

One evening a month, we would attend wrestling at The Corn Exchange in Bury St. Edmunds. This was before wrestling became a TV sport. On such occasions, we saw Jackie Pallo, Masumbula the witchdoctor, Steve Logan, and many more, who later became household names. We even went to an occasional greyhound race meeting in Bury St. Edmunds, as my uncle, Will Hicks, had a greyhound he used to race.

We enjoyed being with each other so much, that in the Summer of 1961, we decided to take a holiday together. We chose one of the Butlins holiday camps situated around the UK which were popular at the time, booking a holiday in Pwllheli, North Wales, for early July. Kate and I weren't even engaged at this point. It was unprecedented for an unmarried couple to holiday together; our parents' approval was very enlightened. A booking was made for separate, albeit adjacent, chalets. Getting to Pwllheli meant a coach journey from Newmarket via London Victoria coach station. Fortunately, Kate's father was a chauffeur for Sir Alfred Butt, a racehorse owner, and he happened to be going to London that day to pick up Sir Alfred. Kate's father drove us to the coach terminus in one of Sir Alfred's cars – a Rolls Royce. The bus journey to North Wales was overnight, so we tried to sleep on the coach until we arrived in Chester, where we had to disembark at 5am and wait two hours for another coach to complete the journey.

Eventually arriving at Butlins in Pwllheli, we checked into our chalets and explored the site. Everything was provided – all the entertainment plus three meals a day in enormous dining halls where we shared a table with six other people. The entertainment and activities were organised by staff called Redcoats, identifiable by the red blazers they all wore. We both joined in as many of the activities as we could – Kate in a talent contest and me in sport. It was a truly memorable week, with so much entertainment laid on. We were sorry to go home.

By the end of 1961, we had known each other for 14 months and were very much in love. We decided to get engaged on Christmas Eve after attending midnight service at All Saints Church in Newmarket. I gave Kate an engagement ring and she gave me a gold signet ring. Our parents were delighted.

The next year, I passed my driving test at the second attempt and purchased a 1947 Austin 8 for £85 – a 4-cylinder with a top speed of about 65mph. I was its fourth owner. The moped Mum had bought me in 1958 I gave to my brother, who had started work as a bricklayer's apprentice. Having a car meant Kate and I could travel together, so it was a real luxury. The car had a sunroof and a windscreen that we could wind out to feel the fresh air on our faces. The drawback was that it had no heater, so in the winter it was very cold. To defrost or demist the windscreen, a metal bar wired to a plug on the dashboard was put on the windscreen with suction pads and plugged into the 6v battery. It took a long time to heat up but did keep the windscreen clear.

This was a time before drink driving laws were introduced, so we would meet up and have a few drinks at The Red Lion, thinking nothing of driving home afterwards. One evening, I attended the darts' team annual dinner on my own as it was a male-only function and drank too many glasses of gin and orange. The journey home from The Red Lion to my parents' house was less than a mile, but I recall hitting the grass verges on both sides of the road on the way, eventually stopping outside the gate at Broad Green. It was not until the early hours that my mother realised I had not come home. When she went outside, she found me drunkenly slumped over the steering wheel. What was even worse was that I had been throwing up in the car, so it was a complete mess. Despite clearing it up the next day, it was a couple of weeks before Kate would get in again due to the smell of vomit! I have not been keen on gin ever since.

The summer of 1962 saw us back on holiday again at Butlins in Pwllheli. This time we booked for two weeks, which was the maximum holiday entitlement we both had from our jobs. We did not fancy the gruelling coach journey again so decided to take my Austin 8. To make sure the car was up to the long trip, Kate's dad checked it over (being a chauffeur, he was incredibly good at understanding the mechanics of a car). The journey took all day, stopping occasionally to rest, but the car never let us down and we enjoyed the journey. As before, we got involved in as many of the activities at the holiday camp as we could and had a fantastic fortnight together. Once the holiday was over, it was back to our jobs – Kate to Boots and me to W.A. Challis.

During the harvest time, if Kate was not attending Cambridge for her singing lessons on her half-day off, she would cycle to whichever field I was working on with the combine harvester, park her bike, cross the field, and climb up the steps of the combine and sit behind me for a couple of hours. Her hair and clothes would get covered in the chaff and dust, as in those days there was no protection – the driver sat in the open air with the noise of the machinery all around.

The winter of 1963 turned out to be the biggest freeze in living memory. It started to snow on Boxing Day 1962, and, that evening, Kate had been at mine for tea. Snow and ice had made the roads treacherous and the only way I could get her home for work the next day was by the tractor with a snowplough! We walked up to Mick Challis's house about a mile away and started up the tractor. The vehicle featured a small cab, so Kate squeezed in beside me and we snowploughed the three miles to her house.

For our next two-week summer holiday together, we decided to go even further afield and choose the Butlins holiday camp at Ayr on the west coast of Scotland. We decided to drive there in the Austin 8. This meant that the car needed to be in exceptional condition, so Kate's dad once again checked it over, changing the brake pads, tyres, and making other adjustments so it was in tiptop condition. As the journey would take two full days, we decided to break it up by staying with Geoff and Pauline, who were now married and living in Manchester. Geoff had obtained his degree and was working for British Petroleum as a chemical engineer. It was a long drive to Manchester and dark by the time we arrived at their house. They were pleased to see us, and, after chatting for a long time, catching up on each other's news, we eventually all went to bed – Kate had her room, and I had mine.

The next day after breakfast, we set off again. For most of the journey we kept to the A6, which was being converted into the M6 motorway in places, so we encountered numerous diversions. Eventually, we arrived at the camp and settled in. Butlins at Ayr was a big holiday camp running down to a lovely, long sandy beach and had all same the facilities we had enjoyed at Pwllheli. This time Kate reached the final of a talent contest singing 'I Could Have Danced All Night' from the musical *My Fair Lady*.

We became friendly with another couple and the four of us jointly entered a competition. By pooling our resources, we produced the most names and addresses to whom we could recommend Butlins as a holiday. My time delivering newspapers and being a bread delivery boy in Cheveley village was a major factor in our success, as I easily remembered all the names and addresses. For this, we won a bottle of champagne and duly celebrated that evening.

As we had the car, we decided to venture further afield. The Island of Arran, just off the Ayrshire coast, could be reached by taking a ferry from Ardrossan on the mainland, so we decided to drive there and see when the next ferry was due. This was before the days of 'roll-on, roll-off' ferries. We parked the car at Ardrossan and boarded the ferry on foot. The island had particular significance for Kate's dad, as he would visit while chauffeuring for Lord Curzon who sometimes holidayed there in the summer. As the ferry arrived at Brodick, the harbour on Arran, there were coaches offering a tour of the island, so we decided to take one. It was a thoroughly enjoyable day and extremely hot. Arran has since become one of my favourite Scottish islands, and I have been back several times during my hillwalking expeditions and weekends away with Kate.

It was to be another 18 months – 6th June 1964 – before we were married at All Saints Church in Newmarket, exactly 20 years after D-Day. I had chosen Derek Smith as my best man, a schoolfriend with whom Kate and I had continued to socialise, together with his fiancée, Pam. For bridesmaids, Kate chose her cousin Stephanie, my sister Jill, and her niece, Angela. Her friend Pauline, who had married Geoff the previous year, was appointed matron of honour. It was a momentous day which went all too quickly, the ceremony followed by a reception at All Saints Church Hall and dancing to the Jack Munns Trio. We had a great sendoff after the reception. Despite hiding my car before the service, it was traditionally decorated and daubed with colours, so as we drove off, our 'just married' status was obvious to everyone. I had booked us into the four-star Angel Hotel in Bury St. Edmunds for our honeymoon night. We were both covered in confetti, so halfway to the hotel, we stopped to brush some of it off and tried to clean up the car, without success. Upon arrival, we left the car outside in the hotel car park and checked in, trying not to look nervous. Neither of us had stayed in such a luxurious hotel before, but all the staff knew we were newlyweds so were kind and welcoming. We were shown to the honeymoon suite with its four-poster bed, and, after such a hectic day, we were alone at last!

The next morning, after breakfast, we had a stroll in Abbey Gardens which were directly opposite the hotel. It was lovely and sunny as we reflected on the previous day, while mindful of our need to be at Cambridge Airport for our flight to Jersey that afternoon, where we were to spend our honeymoon. After the morning walk and a read of the Sunday papers, we drove to Cambridge Airport. Parking the Austin 8, we checked in for our flight. Emerging from the terminal building, we were met by a tremendous welcome. It seemed that everyone who had attended our wedding had come to see us off. As we were called to board the aircraft – a twin-engine Dakota of Derby Airways (latterly becoming British Midland Airways in the 1980s), my mum pressed a tiny St. Christopher into my hand that she had had for many years and wished us good luck.

Neither of us had flown before, so it was with some trepidation that we climbed the steps and settled into our allocated seats. As the aircraft taxied to the runway and we looked out of the window, we could see the wedding guests waving. The plane reached the end of the runway, and, before preparing its run, tested each engine in turn on full power. This was normal practice, but the whole aircraft shook and vibrated. I remembered my dad, who served in the Royal Air Force during the war, saying that Dakotas had functioned as troop carriers during that time and had been the mainstay of the Berlin airlift, so this settled the nerves. Having tested both engines to full power separately, they were now on full power together and we were hurtling down the runway. Within a minute we were airborne, and Cambridge was disappearing fast below us.

The Dakota touched down in Derby (now East Midlands Airport) to board more passengers, before then heading onwards to Jersey. Over the English Channel a handwritten flight report was passed along the plane, informing the passengers that we were at a height of 12,000ft and that the weather in Jersey was sunny. Occasionally, we would hit an air pocket, due to the low level, and the plane would drop several hundred feet before levelling out again. I remember food and drinks being served by a stewardess but cannot remember what we had. The other incident that sticks in my memory is Kate turning her head and one of her contact lenses popping out. Then began a search on the floor to find it, which thankfully we did.

Two-and-a-half hours later, after a stop in Guernsey, we touched down in Jersey. We collected our bags and proceeded to our honeymoon hotel in Gorey Bay, and, for the second time, checked in as Mr and Mrs Nash.

We had a wonderful week in Jersey, with brilliant weather. We hired a Morris 1000 convertible and toured the island. Life could not have been better. Another couple were staying at the hotel – Vic and Sandra from Essex. They were also newlyweds, and we spent a bit of time together relaxing on the white sandy beaches. One day, Vic lost his wedding ring which had come off in the surf on St. Ouen's Bay. Years later, when I started metal detecting as a hobby, I reflected on this occasion. Finding rings on beaches became easy with these modern machines.

We kept in contact with Vic and Sandra. Two years later, in August 1966, the four of us went on a residential caravan holiday in Cromer, courtesy of Sprite Caravans where I now worked. I had won the week's holiday in a prize draw held for employees. We kept in contact with the couple for several years but eventually lost touch.

Almost two years to the day of our wedding, our firstborn, Michaela Jane, was born – 2 June 1966. She was followed by Graham Peter, born

3 February 1969, and, finally, Paul Michael, who was born 6 September 1977 – three great children.

Kate and I celebrated our 25th wedding anniversary at the Royal Hotel Bridge of Allan with family and friends; for our 40th anniversary, we celebrated by taking a cruise on the Hebridean Princess, cruising the western isles of Scotland, the same ship later chartered by the Queen. When the 50th wedding anniversary arrived, we celebrated on the famous Orient Express, journeying from London to Venice, where we stayed for a few days.

We loved each other's company, and both enjoyed travelling and experiencing other cultures. We visited Australia, New Zealand, Fiji, China, Russia, Peru, South Africa, Sri Lanka, Maldives, and the Caribbean, to name but a few. Every November, we would spend four weeks in Madeira enjoying the sunshine and walking the Levadas, escaping the bleak Scottish days when daylight hours were so short. We spent many weekends at Pitlochry Festival Theatre, staying at our favourite place: Green Park Hotel. We combined these weekends with lovely walks around Perthshire.

Kate really got into walking and decided to walk the West Highland Way, 95 miles from Milngavie, near Glasgow, to Fort William. She decided to do this to raise money for the Alzheimer's Society in memory of her sister who had died from the condition. We did this together, staying overnight along the way in B&Bs or hotels. Her choice to do it during June 2011 meant that our 47th anniversary was celebrated with an evening at Rowardennan Hotel, located alongside Loch Lomond, before walking 20 miles the next day to Crainlarich. I was a member of a walking group called Trimarc that helped me complete all the Munros in July 2013. Kate was there alongside me when I did the last one – Beinn na Lap – together with 23 other walking friends and family members. She enjoyed the three-day breaks with Trimarc, visiting many of the Scottish islands and the hills in the Lake District in later years, during the spring and autumn.

Our 56th wedding anniversary came in 2020, the year the global pandemic COVID-19 began, eventually killing over seven million people, 232,112 in the UK. The UK Government imposed a national lockdown and so Kate and I isolated together indoors for over three months, only leaving the house to go for walks. We spent our time together in the garden at Gleniffer, enjoying the glorious unseasonal weather. Many times, during this period, we said how nice it was just enjoying being together without ever having the need to go anywhere.

On 21 June 2020, whilst preparing vegetables for dinner, my darling wife of 56 years suffered a haemorrhagic stroke. Kate was not a 'typical' candidate, the stroke entirely unexpected – no previous symptoms nor signs. I recognised the symptoms she described to me, and I rushed her to the emergency department at Forth Valley Royal Hospital. A scan revealed the worst possible news. Michaela, Graham and Paul were notified and arrived to be with us as soon as they could, Michaela travelling through the night from Winchester. Despite the restrictions imposed by the COVID-19 pandemic, we were all allowed to stay by Kate's bedside, comforting her and playing her some music. Each of the grandchildren spoke to her by mobile phone. The next morning there were signs of some recovery, so she was moved to the specialist stroke ward, where no visitors were allowed. Each day, we communicated with her for 15 minutes via a Skype link using an iPad the ward provided.

Things were beginning to look promising, and we remained hopeful. Then, in the early hours of 30 June, I received a phone call at 4am from her nurse saying she had had a difficult night and suggested I come to the hospital. Michaela was still staying with me, so, waking her up, we quickly got dressed and drove to the hospital, Michaela alerting Graham and Paul as I drove. Despite the COVID-19 restrictions, the ward allowed two of us to stay with Kate at any one time. Another scan revealed there had been further bleeding in her brain, from which she was unlikely to recover. Kate died peacefully at 8.55pm on 1 July 2020 with Michaela and I at her bedside.

I shall for ever miss her – she was an inspiration and supported everything I did. We had known each other for 60 years and been married for just over 56. Kate was a loyal and wonderful wife, a devoted mother to our three children – Michaela, Graham and Paul – and a much-loved grandma to Stuart, Rory, Andrew, Rachael and Clara. I will never, ever forget her. I have some fantastic memories that I hope will sustain me as I face the challenges of the rest of my life without her.

7

SPRITE CARAVANS

The 2nd of November 1968 marked my first day as an operative on a production line building touring caravans for Sprite Caravans.

It was on this dark November morning, armed with a hammer, pliers and junior hacksaw, that I reported to the Sprite factory, known as 'The Oaks', located in Fordham Road, Newmarket. I was to join the operatives on what was known as main line A. In charge, was a shop foreman called Ken Ashwell. After the introductions, he called over one of his chargehands, Ted Ginder, whose team I was to join on the main line assembly.

The noise and bustle of the assembly line was not entirely new, as a few years previously I had visited the Vauxhall motor factory in Luton on a daytrip. However, I was amazed at the amount of activity before me: I watched a basic chassis on wheels become a touring caravan! People worked on their individual tasks, beginning each one as the assembly line moved along.

I was placed with an operator called Michael Kirkby, known as 'Rip', who showed me what to do. Having been made in the chassis shop, each chassis entered the line with a specification document attached, designating the model. The document also stated whether it was being produced for the home or continental market. If it was continental, the ticket would indicate the country to which it would be dispatched upon completion. The model I worked on was a Sprite Alpine, and my job was to assist Rip to screw the floor to the chassis, after it had been placed on it, around the wheel indents. This meant having to drill holes through the floor into the chassis and secure with self-tapping countersunk screws. We then had to secure aluminium, angled plates to the front of the floor ready to take the front end. The final task at this stage was to connect the gas pipe coming up through the floor, to the gas pipe on the side. This supplied the gas wall light and gas hob. All this had to be accomplished in eight minutes as the line moved on – I had to be ready for the next one. At this speed, the total number of completed caravans rolling off the production line each day was 75. Our nine-hour day started at 7.30am, and, during that time, we had a 15-minute tea break at 10am, a 60-minute lunch break at 12.30pm, and a 10-minute tea break at 4pm, finishing at 6pm. This was indeed mass production, and I was now part of it.

My second day was different – instead of working with Rip, I was given a new task as 'riveter'. The model I would be working on that day was a Sprite 400, smaller than the Alpine. The job entailed joining the aluminium panels on the front and back of each caravan using a rivet gun. For this task I had to place a rivet into a rivet gun, which was connected to an air-line, place the head of the rivet into a predrilled hole in the aluminium, and pull the trigger. This action had the effect of squeezing the rivet head, thus joining the panels together. I had around 40 of these to do on each caravan before the next one arrived. Whilst I was doing these, other operatives were working on inserting window trims and fixing the furniture to the interior, which had previously been loaded. This consisted of a sink unit, bunkbeds, roof lockers, and wardrobes – everything needed to turn this basic shell into a travelling home.

As the caravan left my area, it moved down the production line to have the ceiling fitted, which had been preassembled. Over this, went the aluminium roof. Windows were then added, as well as a door, taillights, sidelights, number plate lights, guttering, and trims – according to each model. Finally, the completed caravan arrived at the door of the paint shop where it was firstly degreased, then into the paint bay for spraying the designated model colour. Originally, the company manufactured three models: the Sprite 400, a four-berth; Sprite Alpine, a four-berth that could be six, and Sprite Musketeer, a six-berth. The company later produced a Sprite Cadet, a two-berth that could be towed by a moped.

This was my first time working in a factory, so it was quite a shock to the system after working outside in agriculture. The wages, however, were the best in the Newmarket area, and although I started on 4/7d an hour as a grade C operative, after six weeks, having learned three stages on the production line, I was promoted to grade B, earning 5/5d an hour. I achieved grade A after three months, reaching the top rate of 6/3d an hour. In addition to this, a daily bonus could be earned by a work rate known as 85 prodex, a term used for exceeding a work rate of what would normally be expected in an hour. This was achieved by completing 85 minutes' work in 60 minutes. The whole production line had to achieve this, so it was tough keeping up; if you got behind on your task, you slowed the whole production line down. However, there was great camaraderie and teamwork as someone would jump in and help you, even though they had finished their task, as their bonus was at stake, too.

I made many new friends as we were moved from stage to stage of the production process, often having to work in pairs, especially the assembly of the caravan's front and rear ends. The company held an annual Christmas party at the Carlton (now demolished) in Newmarket attended by Sam Alper, the man who started Sprite Caravans in 1948. It usually ended with him in the middle of the group, dancing to the tune of 'Any Old Iron'. As the company grew, the annual Christmas party was held at the Rowley Mile racecourse building and had well-known celebrities attending, including the popular TV personality of the day, The Singing Postman, from Norwich, famed for singing "Hev Yew Gottta Loight, Boy?'

After two years, I was promoted to the job of 'floater'. This meant I could accomplish every task in the first six stages of production. The purpose of a floater was to relieve people who went for a toilet break or left their station unattended for any other reason, such as being late clocking in. (The production line started promptly at 7.30am and did not stop until 6pm!) This position proved to be more interesting and varied, so the time went quickly. An essential part of this job was to maintain an inventory of spare working drills and tools, so if there was a breakdown, it could quickly be replaced without holding up production, the defective part taken to maintenance for repair. I also learnt to sharpen blunt drill bits on a grinding wheel rather than throw them away, which to this day I still do. Another part of the role was to gather the tea break orders from the canteen for the operatives I floated for, such as filled rolls, cakes, chocolate, and cigarettes. The orders, with payment, were placed at the canteen, then collected later and distributed as required. The floater also had to keep a check on the extras that needed fitting – gas points, water pumps, additional wiring – and be able to carry them out while the production line moved on.

Sprite Caravans was a thriving business and provided the best employment in the Newmarket area, even taking the stable lads away from the racehorse training establishments due to the enhanced earning potential. These touring caravans were not only produced for the home market but for many European and Scandinavian countries as well. At the peak of my time as a floater, over 100 Sprite 400s rolled off the production line every day.

By this time, I had moved football clubs to play for Exning United FC after being persuaded by the player/coach John Parfitt, who was a chargehand in the body shop department of Sprite's. Brian Wood, one of my operative colleagues on the production line, was also the goalkeeper, so too John Hardy who lived opposite me in Heathbell Road. It seemed that everyone with whom I had made friends or knew previously, worked at Sprite's, especially the cricketers and footballers.

On 1 September 1969, I was appointed to the role of supervisor, the new name for what was previously known as a chargehand. My promotion came about through Jimmy Cook, who worked as the chargehand when I was a floater. Jimmy was moving to the panel shop department as shop manager. He had been pleased with my work as his floater and had put my name forward to be one of his supervisors in the panel shop.

The panel shop was the department responsible for making all the items of furniture from the materials that had been cut and shaped by the sawmill department. This was a completely different role for me, overseeing people and a department I knew little about. The promotion, however, meant I was now on a salary rather than paid on an hourly rate. My salary was £1,240 a year plus overtime. In addition, I was eligible for the company's pension scheme, life cover and sick pay.

My first task was to learn the processes by which the panel department operated. There were some large pieces of woodworking machinery I needed to familiarise myself with, as well as assembly jigs and presses. Whilst not expected to operate them, I had to understand what they did in order to supervise the work required.

Every piece of material in timber lengths or sheet panels arrived from the sawmill, cut to the correct size and numbered. From this, a card was made out, detailing what parts of timber were required to make a certain piece of furniture or part of a panel, depending on the model of caravan being made. The panel shop was in effect making the parts of furniture that would then later be moved to the cabinet shop for assembly into the different furniture items for each caravan. The number of operatives in the panel shop numbered around 40, each of whom would assemble these several hundred timber parts into the panels of furniture. For the completed item of furniture to be finished and ready when required by the main line, the panel shop had a lead time over the cabinet shop of at least two days, whilst the cabinet shop had a lead time of a day.

I spent four weeks understanding the processes whilst doing quality checks of the finished panels, checking the sizes after they had been glued, pressed and machined. One machine that edge-banded the sink unit tops always appeared to be giving us problems; the edge band had to be filed down by hand to keep the production line on target. This seemed to me to be a backward step, considering the investment that had been made in this machine. As well as getting to understand how the panel shop functioned, I spent time with the operatives to learn what they were doing, so in the event of an operative's absence, I could reallocate the job to someone who understood the process. I got on very well with them all; there was no hostility towards me having come from another department. Jimmy Cook, the shop manager, was also fortunate in that he took over the department while retaining a supervisor named Edward Cooper, whose knowledge and experience was so valuable.

I made good progress, and in October was given the responsibility for the operatives who made the frame assemblies for the bed bunks. I was really enjoying the role, but on 5 November, while playing in a floodlit football match for Exning United at West Row, I went in for a tackle and broke the tibia and fibula of my right leg. I couldn't return to work until early March 1969 when the surgeon discharged me.

During my four-month absence, I received tremendous support from all the operatives in the panel shop with cards and get-well messages, as well as offers to pick me up to take me to social functions. Les Hockley, being my next-door neighbour, also kept me up to date and would take me to evening events. As a staff member, I continued receiving my monthly salary, which at the time was extremely helpful.

When I did return, I found it difficult at first to pick up from where I had left off as some changes had been made. However, everyone was very patient, and, in a couple of weeks, it felt as though I had never been away.

For a further two years, the panel shop became my working life. During this time, staff changes meant two more supervisors were promoted: Eddie Bond and Derek Smith joined me in the panel shop. Derek had been best man at my wedding so his appointment at work was a real bonus. Eddie was also a great guy to work with, always full of hilarity. One of his favourites was a running joke he did for the new people who joined the company. He'd grab hold of an overhead girder and swing from it, making a sound like a monkey. To the startled newcomers, he'd quip, "Stay here too long, mate, it gets you like this!"

A short time after Derek and Eddie joined me, Jimmy Cook was transferred to another department, and John Ginder became shop manager. John was the younger brother of Ted Ginder, who had been my first chargehand in November 1968. John, an exceptionally good footballer, had also been in the team playing for Exning United the night I broke my leg. John had a different style of managing to Jimmy Cook, but, nevertheless, we all gelled, and the panel shop functioned well.

For its supervisors, the company organised internal and external courses, each time with the intention of educating us how to better perform the role. Industrial relations were starting to change, so being able to understand behaviour and avoid flashpoints was essential. I benefitted from this when I formed my own limited company in 1991.

Sprite's sent me on a management supervisory course on a day release basis. I attended West Suffolk College in Bury St. Edmunds in 1972 and eventually obtained the Certificate in Supervisory Studies. The course included a two-night residential stay (4–5th March) at the Marlborough Hotel in Felixstowe, Suffolk. Two years later, I attended the advanced course which included a four-day residential in Rotterdam, Holland. I obtained the advanced certificate. This included the specialised subject of cost control – an important subject which years later I was to benefit from when I changed jobs.

The Sprite courses were enjoyable learning opportunities, especially the one in Rotterdam where I saw how other businesses operated. Both courses were a year in duration and included a project chosen by the works manager. My projects were 'Investigating security within the plant regarding raw materials' and 'Investigating the efficiency of 'indirects' between the sawmill and the panel shop'. These projects had to be researched, and my recommendations typed up. Before the days of word processors and photocopiers, this was quite a task to fit in with work and home life.

In 1974/5 we went through the 'Winter of Discontent' caused by the coal miners' strike. Coal production had ceased, meaning no coal was being provided to the power stations to generate electricity. To conserve the dwindling coal stocks, electricity supplies were regulated to factories and businesses so that homes could be kept supplied. All power stations were reliant on coal to provide the power, so at a certain time each day, the power was shut down and everything stopped. This action meant production would be lost as the whole factory was powered by electricity. Sam Alper, an entrepreneur, solved this problem by hiring large generating units from local fairgrounds that could be started up and plugged into the factory supply, thereby keeping everything going. Homes were later also regulated, with power being cut off for two hours in the evening.

From time to time, I was seconded to other roles, spending time on C line which produced a more upmarket model of the 400. This model had the side frames filled with foam instead of fibreglass. The foam had to be injected by mixing chemicals, after calculating the space to be filled – very similar to insulating cavity walls of houses, where this technique was originally used. As this process was continuous, it meant me doing some shiftwork. I had only ever worked during daylight hours, so starting work at 10pm and finishing at 6am was at first very strange. But one soon got used to sleeping until 2pm, then the whole day was free until 10pm. On quiet nights, if everything was going well, it gave me the opportunity to make toys for the children: a box with sections for the children's Lego pieces survives to this day, as well as a multistorey car park for Graham's Matchbox cars and a desk for Michaela. All this I made from scrap materials using the various available machines.

I was also drafted into the department that produced the prototypes for the new models to be made the following year. This lasted around six weeks and was an interesting experience, seeing how a new model became a reality from a drawing.

One year, several caravans developed some defects with the exterior aluminium panels, so volunteers were called to work at weekends to correct them by replacing the panels. I volunteered as it meant extra money. It took just over six weeks to complete the task, and the only time I had off was when playing football on Saturday afternoons.

Working in a factory environment was demanding, with deadlines to meet, but the camaraderie was magnificent. Each department had a workers' committee member who met monthly with the management to discuss any difficulties and problems. This worked effectively, until trade unions saw an opportunity to recruit members, and began wanting to call strikes over the slightest disagreement. There was a move to recruit the supervisors and foreman to the Association Scientific Technical and Managerial Staff (ASTMS) over some minor issue, which I cannot now remember. To me, the move was unnecessary, as senior management had always been fair in sorting out disputes with production staff and supervisors. With over 900 workers at one plant, such disputes were inevitable.

In early May 1974, I had received a letter from Ernest H. Draycott, the manager of Barclays Griffin Life Assurance, Cambridge office, stating that the company was seeking to recruit representatives who could speak to likeminded sportspeople and other youngsters about the savings and investments available from the company. I later learned that this letter had been sent to all Class One football referees who were listed in the Suffolk County Football Association Handbook.

The opportunity appealed to me, and, after discussions with Kate, who by then had resumed her own career as a dispensing assistant, albeit part-time, we decided I should attend an interview at the Cambridge district office to find out more. The interview was with Mr Draycott, an ex-army major and himself a former Class One football referee. The job entailed speaking not only to sportspeople and youngsters, but members of the public who may wish to save money or invest for their future. The company was offering £100 per month, guaranteed for nine months, then commission only.

The job sounded interesting, and as I had become disillusioned with the involvement of the trade unions at Sprite Caravans, who caused more disputes than resolutions, together, Kate and I decided that if I were offered the job following the interview, I would accept it.

I received a contract in the post two weeks later, signed, and returned it.

So it was, that after nine years and seven months, just five months short of getting a cruet set for ten years' service, I cycled home from Sprite Caravans on 24 May 1974, having given a month's notice. I left without a fanfare – without any good luck messages, cards or a farewell party, which was disappointing. Only Peter Fussey, the section manager, took the trouble to see me on my last afternoon to give his personal best wishes.

I was leaving Sprite's for a completely new career as a representative of Barclays Griffin Life Assurance Society, a subsidiary of Barclays Bank. This proved to be a good decision as Sprite's later ceased to exist.

Sprite Caravans was once the biggest employer in Newmarket, at its peak employing over 900 people[1]. However, during the early 1980s, people's needs changed, with package holidays abroad guaranteeing sunshine. Consequently, caravan sales started to decline. Numbers of caravans manufactured were reduced, and, despite many changes and efforts, including a revamp of the models and factory changes, after sustaining losses of £3.2m in 1981, Sprite Caravans was placed into the hands of receivers. The remaining 200 workers were made redundant.

1 *The Story of Sprite Caravans*, Andrew Jenkinson, Veloce Publishing Limited, 2011, ISBN 978-1845843588

8

BARCLAYS LIFE

Within a few days of leaving Sprite Caravans, I found myself sitting in a training room at 252 Romford Road, London, on 3 June 1974 with 16 other people, learning how to sell life assurance. This location was the head office of Barclays Griffin Life Assurance Company, soon to be renamed Barclays Life, part of Barclays Bank Group PLC.

The course I was now on was two weeks of intensive technical and sales training, learning the various products and techniques to secure sales. This was a complete change for me, as it was for the other course candidates, who were from different areas of the UK. Alex Russell, a refereeing colleague from Lakenheath, was also on the course. He was a carpenter joiner but, like me, had decided to change careers. As the course was residential, we stayed in London hotels for the whole two weeks and only returned at the weekend.

On completion of the course, Alex Russell and I were told that Bill Tee, who was to be our supervisor, would contact us the following Monday. Sure enough, the telephone rang, and Bill Tee introduced himself. He said, "Congratulations, you have got yourself a marvellous job!" Bill, a former Gurkha, had been in the company for just over two years. He requested I attend a meeting he was holding the next day as it would be an opportunity to meet other members he also supervised and get some sales ideas. The meeting was held at his home in Widdington, a village near Saffron Walden.

At the meeting it was apparent that the other members of his team were having different degrees of success. The meeting concluded after about two hours. Now in possession of a rate book, various product booklets and sales materials, I was qualified to advise on various savings plans offered by the company.

The saving plans were known as unit linked and had been pioneered by Mark Weinberg of Hambro Life. It involved people saving a monthly amount into a savings plan linked to a unit trust. Part of the monthly amount saved was invested into the chosen unit trust, the remainder used to provide life assurance. As life assurance was part of the plan, the whole premium attracted tax relief at 17.5% – effectively, the life assurance was paid for by the tax relief element. It was quite a brilliant concept and extremely attractive, if you could persuade people to grasp the concept and take out a plan.

Previously, the traditional life companies like Pearl, Prudential, Co-op, and others had had the market to themselves. I already had a traditional life policy, taken out with the London & Manchester when I was 21. However, the advantage of the unit linked plan was that instead of relying on bonuses being added, as decided by the life company, your monthly premium would purchase units in a unit trust or linked fund every month. The potential for savings to grow was greater, due to the pound cost averaging concept. (A regular investment every month averages out fluctuations rather than trying to predict the correct time to invest.) You could also look up the unit prices in the daily newspaper to monitor progress.

Upon seeing the opportunity, I was filled with optimism: it was known that some established representatives were earning good money. There were two main recommendations for obtaining what were known as 'prospects': cold calling in person or compiling lists from categories in the yellow pages of the telephone directory –

joiners, plumbers, farmers, and tradesmen. The objective was to obtain an appointment, so you could do your sales presentation from a script you had been given at the training course.

Only having 'sold' apples during the lunch break at Sprite's to earn a few extra pennies, this type of selling was a completely new ball game for me. I always prefer to speak to people in person, so I decided to use the cold calling method. I chose a newly developed area to target, my reasoning being that it would be inhabited by people with young families with a need to save for the future, an element of life assurance paid for by the tax relief. Fourteen miles away was a new town called Haverhill, built after the Second World War to rehouse people whose homes were destroyed, and also to address the general housing deficit following the war. My plan was not particularly successful, however; from cold calling over 100 people, I did make one or two sales which gave me some encouragement.

The first six months can best be described as a struggle and apart from the guaranteed money from the company, it was fortunate Kate was now also earning again. However, I continued to make progress by selling to friends, sport colleagues and family who were keen to help me progress and believed in the concept of the unit linked savings plans. I even tried selling in Guernsey whilst on holiday with the family when we stayed with Kate's parents, who had since moved there.

It was much later that I learned the many representatives who were successful were provided with leads from the Barclays Bank branches to which they were allocated. This privilege, however, was not available until you proved you could be a success without this support. The breakthrough for me came one late October evening in 1974, when my supervisor, Bill Tee, called me about five o'clock to ask if I could do his appointments. He had arranged these the week before – referrals from the Soham branch of Barclays Bank. Bill had been playing golf that day and returned to the clubhouse for a few drinks, having more than he should. He was therefore incapable of fulfilling the appointments.

It would reflect badly on him if he had to cancel, or else attend intoxicated. So, he asked me. I managed to get all the names and addresses from him and duly fulfilled the appointments. Of the four appointments, I either sold a savings plan or lump sum Barclays bond investment, proving myself capable of handling the bank's customers.

Within a month, Ernie Draycott had allocated me the following Barclays Bank branches to work with: Haverhill, Newmarket, Soham, and Burwell. Later, more were to follow, extending as far as Downham Market, St Ives, and Chatteris. The only drawback with the bank introductions was that I only received 50% of the commission, the other half going to the branch that had its own targets to achieve. Nevertheless, if you obtained referrals from these successes, it was more than worthwhile.

I was now thoroughly enjoying the job and starting to earn some good commissions, which was fortunate as the company guarantee had now ceased. Most of the appointments were in the evenings, so during the day I would take Michaela and Graham to school and collect them when they finished. In between, I would do the gardening, paint, and decorate, and, in the summer, I would act as groundsman for the cricket pitch in Newmarket where I was also captain.

In 1976, I won the Ipswich region's Winter Incentive Award for getting the most business. For this, Kate and I were invited to London for a celebration dinner at the Tower Hotel on 12 March, hosted by the sales manager and directors. We joined all the other regional winners. As well as the award, I received a £100 voucher to spend at Russell's, the London jewellers.

Whilst this success was being achieved, the regional office had moved from Cambridge to Ipswich. Ernie Draycott, my manager, had retired, and George Goshawk replaced him, relocating the office to Norwich. At the same time, Bill Tee stepped down as supervisor and Clyde Wilson became my group controller (as they were now known). Clyde was West Indian and had an impatient attitude. We did, however, get along okay and would be invited to his house near Norwich as a family to dine with him and his family on occasional Saturday evenings.

After another year, it was all change again as the company changed the regional areas and I was moved to a new office in Market Deeping, near Peterborough. This location had been chosen by the new manager, Ted Green, who lived in Rutland. It meant I had to leave the group under Clyde Wilson and join a new group controller – Rod Cowlin. This, however, did not last long as Rod ended up leaving a few months later after having an affair with a female group controller from another region. Ted Green informed me of this incident and told me he'd put my name forward to replace Cowlin as group controller.

By now, I knew the role of group controller quite well and said I would be pleased to take on the role, if accepted. This would mean attending an interview in London with the sales manager, Peter Horrocks. Afterwards, I thought the interview had gone well and, sure enough, on 1 October 1978, I was appointed group controller of the Peterborough district office. The job entailed a weekly meeting with district manager, Ted Green, in the Market Deeping office, to discuss the progress of the group under my control. My job included assisting with recruitment interviews for new representatives, managing my group members and providing sales support to them daily, and attending the regional training week in Birmingham once a month to teach and train new recruits. The job was very demanding, but a company car was provided, and I would receive an 11% override on my group's earnings, as well as generate commission from my own sales, when time allowed.

The area I covered went as far north as Northampton, as far east as Downham Market, and as far west as Huntingdon. I had nine representatives to look after and tried to spend one day a month with each of them. I also had to liaise with the Barclays Bank branches in all those areas to receive the names of prospective customers who may wish to take out a plan.

For the first time, I was able to save money on a regular basis and I opened an account with the Gateway Building Society. We moved to a larger house on 14 January 1977, so that I had a study to work from. We had also added to our family, Paul born on 6 September 1977. Life was going well, as that same year I had captained Newmarket Cricket Club to the Suffolk Division One championship.

On 31 March 1978, Kate and I were invited to London when my group won the Winter Incentive Award. Once more, we had dinner with the other winners and the directors at the Tower Hotel. I received another £100 to spend at Russell's.

During my successful training days at the Birmingham regional office, where I had been teaching new recruits and imparting my success, I had impressed Alan Gibbins, the regional manager's assistant, and the regional manager, Barry Robinson. Alan was the course leader, but Barry Robinson sometimes sat in. I was invited to speak about my success at the next Midland regional conference due to be held in Buxton, Derbyshire on 6 July 1978. I approached this with some trepidation but worked hard on my speech and made sure I rehearsed it well the night before. It was well received by the regional representatives, and I got lots of praise. I had based my speech on the need to budget and how much one needed to earn. Once this was known, the average commission needed for each plan was then divided, so you knew how many plans you needed to sell. Allowing for a 10% lapse ratio, you then knew how many plans you needed to sell in a year. Removing weekends and holidays, it worked out at three new plans a week (or one every other day). I also gave the audience some tips on recordkeeping, and sales hints.

On October 6, 1979, my mum died of cancer aged only 62. She had been ill for two years, having had an operation to remove a growth from her thyroid gland. This was a sad time for our family. The evening following her death, I kept the appointments I had made previously as I knew she would not have wanted me to let anyone down. It was difficult and my heart was not in it – I did not make any sales and was glad to get back home.

Two weeks later, I learned that Alan Gibbins was being promoted to manager of the Leicester branch, so the vacancy of regional manager's assistant, based in Birmingham, was available. The regional manager, Barry Robinson, had approached my manager, Ted Green, about me applying for the job.

Once again Kate and I discussed the opportunity – a Barclays Bank staff position with a guaranteed salary, company car, pension, private healthcare and share options. If I got the job, it would mean moving from Newmarket to the Midlands for easy access to the Birmingham office. We agreed that I should apply. Now Mum was no longer with us, we could move away, something she would have been totally against as she loved having her children and grandchildren close by.

Kate and I travelled to London on 13 November 1979 for my final interview with the general manager, David Chitty, at Barclays Unicorn head office, Juxon House, near St Paul's. Whilst I went in for the interview, Kate wandered around the cathedral. After an hour, I met up with Kate and told her that I had been successfully appointed as the regional manager's assistant for the Midlands.

We returned home and immediately began contacting estate agents in the Midlands for details of properties in and around Birmingham. We had even started selecting potential places, when I was asked to attend a further meeting with Peter Horrocks, the sales manager, who was coming into the Peterborough office. At the meeting he asked if I would prefer the RMA's job in Manchester, this vacancy having now also arisen. I replied that if I was going to move away from Newmarket, it really made no difference. So, I left the meeting having now been appointed RMA to Barclays life office in Manchester, reporting to Graham Kenward, the regional manager. Once again, we contacted estate agents for potential properties, this time in the Manchester area.

It was now early December. I was still doing my group controller's role, but my group knew I was going to be moving up north. I decided to hold a Christmas dinner for them at a venue just outside of Cambridge. It turned out to be a great evening, appreciated by them, though tinged with sadness. They really were a good group and had responded well to my managing style, as evidenced by us winning the regional award the year earlier.

As Christmas drew near, we settled on a property in Poynton, Cheshire, and made an offer, which was accepted. There was no problem with having to firstly sell our property in Newmarket, as Barclays Bank provided interest-free bridging facilities, as well as paying for all our removal costs.

We travelled up as a family to see the house before Christmas and were pleased with what we saw. Poynton was in the county of Cheshire on the border of what was then Greater Manchester, with easy motorway access into the city where I would be based. Opposite the house was Poynton Cricket Club's ground, which also featured on the property choice. We would not be moving up until after Easter as schooling for Michaela and Graham had to be considered.

I would, however, be taking up my new role as RMA for the Northern region on 2 January 1980.

9

BARCLAYS LIFE
MANCHESTER

On Monday 2nd January 1980, I left home early for the drive to Manchester. Parking the Fiat 131 Mirafiori on a side street in the city centre, I found the Barclays Life regional office, where I was to be based, and reported to Graham Kenward.

Graham was a larger-than-life character who had been the Northern regional manager for about two years. He had elevated the region from a poorly producing one, to now competing for the top position. He had a reputation for working hard and playing hard and had a noticeably young team of district managers reporting to him. The Northern region consisted of Liverpool, Leeds, Preston, Newcastle, Manchester and Scotland. My role as RMA was to assist the region in developing more salespeople. This would be achieved by helping with the interview process (once a district manager had recommended someone). After this, I would then be organising and running a sales training course once a month. I was also required to be available for one-to-one field sales training, should a district manager need me to spend a day with a salesperson who was performing below par.

My first task was to get to know each district manager, as well as the group controllers. To do this, during my first week Graham had organised a meeting at the De Trafford Arms Hotel in Alderley Edge. I was given a slot on the agenda to introduce myself and to speak about the Barclays Bank liaison, something that had been successful in my previous areas but had not yet been trialled in the North. Having been a group controller and spoken previously at the Midlands Regional Conference as well as at Midlands training courses, I found presentations easy, and my delivery went down well with the managers. They asked a lot of questions about the bank liaison. They were also intrigued to learn how I had joined the industry. When I told them, they then wanted my help to recruit in the same way, asking me to provide names of Class One referees in Cheshire and Lancashire.

Following this meeting, I was then expected to visit each of the districts. So that all the salespeople could get to know me personally, I attended meetings with the district representatives. My first district visit was to Newcastle, which took place over two days – 9 and 10 January. I drove north from Manchester and was introduced to the Newcastle team by the manager, John Waterworth. I stayed at the Swallow Hotel in Newcastle and quickly learned what life could be like in the North East: when I came down to breakfast the next morning, it was to find a large police presence in attendance. Apparently, someone had unfortunately been stabbed just outside the hotel during the night.

I returned to Manchester after that meeting and started to prepare for my first training course the following week. A decision had been taken to combine this meeting with the Midlands district, set to be held at the Post House Hotel in Walsall, starting Monday, 14 January. This course would be run jointly by myself and Steve Ireland, the regional manager's assistant for the Midlands, who, like me, had just been appointed.

Steve was an Irishman with a great sense of humour; we got on well together. Despite our different teaching styles, we complemented each other, and the training course was deemed a success. Staying in the same hotel as the trainees was quite tiring, as I was constantly being asked about the role of a Barclays Life representative and what makes one successful. However, commuting from Newmarket to Walsall was a much shorter journey than having to travel back to Manchester.

A few days later, on 18 January, I attended the Liverpool district meeting, which was held at the Adelphi Hotel. I was familiar with this venue as I had attended the National Referees Conference in my capacity as secretary of Suffolk County Referees Association two years prior. It was one of Liverpool's premier hotels, so I looked forward to going again. Bill Jacklin was the district manager, and I was on the agenda to provide some knowledge and ideas to his team of representatives. The meeting was a success; I easily fitted in with everyone and looked forward to further visits. One of their representatives promised to take me to Anfield, the home of Liverpool Football Club. The promise was honoured, and a few weeks later, my eldest son Graham and I saw Liverpool play against Manchester City and experienced what it was like to be in the famous Kop stand with the Liverpool supporters.

I returned to Manchester after a weekend at home with my family. Back at work, I had a debrief with Graham Kenward, who said that now I had cut my teeth on the course in Walsall as a joint venture, he was keen for me to establish my own course for the coming February. This would be held at Radbroke Hall, near Knutsford. Radbroke Hall was in the Cheshire countryside and had been bought by Barclays Bank many years ago to be used exclusively for the various training courses the bank ran for its staff. It had once been a country estate, covering many acres of beautiful grounds, some of which had now been changed into sports facilities for games including cricket and football. Graham Kenward arranged for me to meet Les Moore who was based at Radbroke Hall. He held the title Assistant Field Manager. Les was close to retiring and it seemed to me he was like a minister without portfolio – I could not understand what his role was. However, he was a lovely man and invited me for lunch in the manager's dining room. This was a very exclusive area of the hall, reserved for managers and their guests. I felt quite privileged as I sipped a gin and tonic, choosing from a nice menu. During lunch, Les asked me how I would be running the courses, as apparently my predecessor had not done very well. I outlined my ideas, which he liked. He said he would like to do a session on the last day of each course which would be of motivational input.

When I went back into the Manchester office the next day, Graham asked me how I had got on. I explained that I had found Les helpful, showing me as he did Radbroke Hall and the training facilities I would be using. I told Graham that I was extremely impressed by the facilities and the training equipment, which was very modern at the time. I would have no problem using the video cameras to record mock sales presentations nor the projectors to show sales training films. He then asked me to set out a course agenda for the week's training course, asking that I ensure Les Moore was not part of it. I could easily put together the agenda as I had previous experience of the course content as a group controller in the Midlands. However, to be told to exclude Les Moore from the programme's agenda seemed odd, especially given he was based at Radbroke Hall as assistant field manager and had been so helpful to me. I later learned that Les had been Manchester district manager before the arrival of Graham Kenward. Soon after, Les had been replaced by Tony Hodgson from Hull who had been promoted. Graham did not think much of Les Moore as a district manager, which was how he ended up at Radbroke Hall.

My next task was to secure accommodation for the new recruits while attending the week's training course. Though Radbroke Hall was a wonderful training centre and had dining faculties, it had no accommodation. This meant that hotels around the Knutsford area benefited by being able to provide bed, breakfast, and evening meals. I decided to reconnoitre the area to research the options. It appeared that The Swan at Knutsford was the most popular but also the most expensive and I had a limited budget. I eventually managed to strike a deal with the owner of a private hotel, The George, which was based in Knutsford high street. It was a former coaching inn with lots of character features. The owner was delighted by our agreement: for one week, every month, he was guaranteed 10–15 guests. It was a delightful place, so much so, I ended up staying there from Monday to Friday whilst commuting from Newmarket.

Having now established the accommodation and the course content, which would include visits and contributions from district managers, group controllers, plus any other successful individuals, all the preparations for the week's training course were complete.

As I got to know each district and how it functioned, I became a regular attendee at district meetings. These were held once a month. My next district was Manchester, conveniently located within the same building as the regional office. The manager, Tony Hodgson, had been successful in recruiting a team of around 25 representatives and three group controllers. He had also had the most successful salesperson in the Northern area: Alan Brough. I do not remember much about the meeting's content, but I do recall giving a talk on my background and some sales tips for obtaining referrals. The meeting was held on a Friday afternoon, and, when it concluded, everyone went to a local pub called Brahams and Liszt (now a restaurant known as Panama Hatty's). I was invited to join them and discovered that this was a Northern tradition after finishing work on a Friday. It meant that if I was in the regional office on a Friday, I would invariably end up joining them for a drink, staying until about 7pm. It was during these occasions when I met Jean Band, one of the female sales representatives. Jean was 33 and single. She lived with her mother as her father had died of cancer when she was in her 20s. She was not as successful as she should be, so Tony Hodgson, her manager, asked me to spend a day in the field with her to see if I could increase her sales figures.

Jean lived in Bolton, so this was where we arranged to meet. It was my first visit to this former mill town, its name only previously known to me in relation to its football team in the famous Matthews Final at Wembley, 1953 – Bolton versus Blackpool. I observed Jean presenting at a couple of appointments, which went quite well despite her being nervous doing them in front of me. After this, I suggested we did some cold calling, an area of the job she admitted not being particularly good at. She said the most difficult people to cold call were traders on Bolton Market, so that is where I said we should go. After a couple of hours speaking to various traders, with some success in getting her appointments, it was lunchtime. We found a local pub for a bar lunch and chatted about the town of Bolton. She said that she had lived in Bolton all her life – both her parents had worked in the mills. She had a brother who worked for Barclays Bank. Jean had a secretarial background, previously employed by the Inland Revenue. Whilst working there, she had been seconded to their London office for a while. Jean told me she had been engaged to be married to another Inland Revenue employee but had called the wedding off at the last minute, despite having paid a deposit for a bungalow. It was a sad story, her deciding he was not the person for her, when all the wedding plans were in place. She thought that all their friends at work had assumed they would marry, and the couple had felt pressured into it. She said it was a relief when she told her parents she was not going through with it. Her father had agreed.

I felt quite privileged that she had shared this story with me, surely for her a traumatic event at the time. As far as I am aware, to this day she never told any of her colleagues in the Manchester district. I felt she had considered me a good friend, someone she could use as a sounding board, especially since losing her father so young. After that day, whenever the opportunity arose, we would have a drink together and I would share more sales ideas with her. She remains a good friend to this day.

The two-day Northern Regional Sales Conference was scheduled to take place in Blackpool in March. In early February, Graham announced we were visiting the Imperial Hotel in Blackpool to negotiate a package with the conference and banqueting manager. The Imperial Hotel was a very prestigious venue and had been used for several years by the main political parties for their annual conferences. Upon meeting the conference manager, Graham proceeded to outline what was required and how many delegates would be attending, plus the number of bedrooms we would need reserving. I contributed my thoughts on the format as I had some knowledge of sales conferences after attending the Midlands and the national ones, which had been held in my first year with the company. Having outlined the company's expectations, Graham then revealed his budget and asked the conference manager if he could work within it. The manager asked us to accompany him to a private lunch to discuss the details. During the lunch, I realised what a superb negotiator Graham was and wondered afterwards whether the Imperial Hotel made any profit from the event. Having agreed the amount, which from memory was around £5,000 for the two-day event, Graham then said, "Of course, the price does also include a weekend for my six managers and their wives later in the year?" I was amazed by his nerve, and even more amazed when the manager agreed! The deal was sealed over several rounds of brandy and coffees. I was not a brandy drinker so felt quite unsteady by the time we left to return to Manchester. Though Graham was less inebriated than me, he should not have driven us back to Manchester, the drink driving limit having come into force in 1967. I had parked my car in the city centre but could not remember exactly where, so, summoning a taxi, I asked the driver to drive me around until I spotted the area where I had left it. Eventually I saw it near the Arndale Centre, which I remembered as the landmark. I was still not completely fit to drive but knew I had to get to the George Hotel in Knutsford where I was staying. I made it safely back and went straight to bed. Awaking during the night, I was aware of my heart beating rapidly due to the excess alcohol and coffee and felt extremely hot. I opened the bedroom window and gulped in the cold air for several minutes until I felt better. The next morning, I missed breakfast but made sure I was on time to the office.

I spent just over a year working in the Manchester region. In early 1981, the Barclays Life Scotland manager left suddenly. As the RMA, I was asked to perform caretaker manager duties at the office in Glasgow until someone else was appointed. This involved commuting to Scotland on a Monday and returning on a Friday, staying in hotels during the week. A novelty at first, as time wore on, it became tiresome. Jenny Perris, the office secretary, did her best to make me feel welcome. She used to bring me homemade soup on a Monday and made the most wonderful tablet (Scottish name for fudge) for me to take home to the children. Jenny was a lovely lady who had lost her husband, suddenly, only two years earlier. She retired in 1983 and moved down to Langholm, a village in the Scottish Borders, to be near her daughter. I kept in touch and once visited her when I was in Langholm. She proudly had on display a photograph of us both taken at the 1981 Barclays Life conference at Turnberry.

Later that year, after regularly commuting back and forth, I was asked to attend another interview in London with David Chitty, the general manager of Barclays Life. Kate came with me again and we spent the day in London. At the interview, I was asked if I would like to apply for the position of Barclays Life District Manager Scotland. The reasoning behind the request was that the Barclays Life management – from the regional manager, sales manager and general manager – had all received good reports of my role as caretaker manager and how well I had related to the salespeople there. I came away from the interview feeling flattered, stating that I would discuss the position further with my wife and get back to them.

Discussing the opportunity, we had to consider that we had only recently moved (April 1980) and settled in Poynton. Another move so soon would be disruptive for us all, especially for Michaela and Graham's education. However, after some discussion, we decided I should formally apply for the position which would commence on 1 January 1981. It was just a formality, really, after Peter Horrocks, the sales manager, met with us and described the opportunity. I would be a Barclays Bank, manager grade employee. This meant an enhanced salary, pension benefits, private health care, and a better company car.

The task for us now was to find a suitable location to live in Scotland within commuting distance of Glasgow.

10

BARCLAYS LIFE
SCOTLAND

I received confirmation of my appointment as district manager for Barclays Life Scotland on 12 November 1981 from the board of Barclays Unicorn Group. This was followed by many letters of congratulations from colleagues and managers I had worked with, not only in the Northern region but the other regions as well. No one was more pleased than the Scotland secretary, Jenny Perris, as it had removed the uncertainty of who would be appointed.

I continued to commute as I had done as the RMA, but now I had the authority and responsibility of budgets, decision-making and the recruitment of more salespeople. The team I inherited could be described as 'ageing' – most in their late 50s or early 60s – and, in most cases, this was a second career they didn't take too seriously. I had got to know the team well during my time as RMA caretaker manager. Jenny provided good feedback on them all and very helpfully got me settled into the role. In total, I had responsibility for three group controllers and seven other salespeople – all males except Carmen Capaldi. Thus far, collectively, their sales of the Barclays Life products could only be described as mediocre.

As a member of the Life Insurance Association (LIA), I attended a meeting soon after my appointment in Glasgow where I met managers of the other established Life companies. Most were from England like me but had settled in Scotland and were now managing successful teams in the cities of Glasgow, Edinburgh, Dundee and Aberdeen. It was after two of these monthly meetings that a plan came to mind: to recruit more younger salespeople outside the major cities, instead of trying to compete with the established life insurance companies already there, such as Abbey Life, Hambro Life, Confederation Life, and Save & Prosper, to name but a few. Unlike the rest of the UK, Barclays Life Scotland had no bank liaison upon which to rely, as there were only three Barclays Bank branches in Scotland: Aberdeen, Edinburgh and Glasgow. There was, however, a link with Barclaycard and Mercantile Credit that could be used for introductions, but this had yet to be agreed. Barclays Unicorn also had a representative – a former army colonel called Jimmy Ferguson who lived in Edinburgh.

So began a recruitment campaign, advertising in local newspapers and magazines, and job centres. The strategy paid off; I found myself busy interviewing potential salespeople. I had also delegated the recruitment duties to group controllers whose interest it was to expand their team, as they received 10% of the commission earned. In the first year, I doubled the sales team and production by recruiting people from further afield: John Doherty from Fort William, Pat Hyatt from Dumfries, George Donald from Lossiemouth, Martin O'Reilly from Kingussie, Andy Donaghy from Auchterarder, and Frank Murdoch from Kilmarnock. David Smart, one of the most successful younger salespeople, introduced Mian Sadiq who was taken on despite a struggle to obtain references. He had a PhD in nuclear physics and had worked on a nuclear fission programme in Pakistan. As it turned out, Mian proved to be the most successful recruit. David also introduced Ben Swinburne from Lanark, who had recently been made redundant and was looking for a change of career. Bill Stephen, who lived in Aberdeen, was also a successful appointment, making regular trips over to Orkney to get business there.

I mention these people specifically because they were the most successful; there were others, who, though showed early promise, later failed. This was to be expected, as, selling a promise (the life policy promises to pay out on the death of the policyholder) was not everybody's cup of tea. I tried to increase the female presence, but those recruited failed to succeed. Carmen Capaldi remained the star female performer. Jean Band came to Scotland during a branch meeting to spend a couple of days with Carmen to learn her sales techniques. Jean was successful at selling single premium bonds but struggled with monthly premium contracts.

Whilst I was busy building the team, Kate and the children remained at home in Newmarket. They came up during the Easter break and we spent four days at the Stakis Dunblane Hydro Hotel deciding where to live and getting to know the area. Kate had spotted a cottage for sale just outside Dunblane on the A9. The cottage was called Capalt Burn. The current owners used it as a showroom for an advertising firm as well as a domestic dwelling. It had four potential bedrooms, a large lounge, another sitting room, two bathrooms, and a kitchen, which needed a lot of refurbishing. The property was surrounded by a large garden with a burn running through it. Of the properties we had seen so far, this was the most attractive. We commissioned a survey that revealed a few defects, especially the kitchen, which was described as 'old-fashioned'. The agent put a market value on the property of £45,000 and advertised it as offers over £52,000. We loved the house; the only drawback was the busy A9 trunk road running parallel to the front of the property. However, we decided to make an offer and put in a price of £46,000. Surprisingly, our offer was accepted.

The city of Dunblane was an ideal location as it was within easy reach of the motorway network for Glasgow and Edinburgh, plus it was on the road north for Aberdeen. It also had a railway station that ran frequent trains to the main cities.

One of the privileges of being a member of bank staff was the preferential mortgage facility they offered. This was made available to staff due to the constant need to move around the country at the behest of the bank. We had only just sold the property in Newmarket; now the property in Poynton was to be sold after just one year.

Capalt Burn needed a lot of decoration, so, after work, each weekday evening I would forgo dinner at the hotel where I was staying to drive to Dunblane, don my overalls, and paint. Most of the walls were covered in woodchip so a coat of paint was easy to apply. Moben Kitchens were chosen to supply new units to upgrade the outdated kitchen, together with a dishwasher, washing machine and dryer, courtesy of Barclays Bank who paid as part of the removal allowance.

We were unable to move until Michaela and Graham had broken up for the school holidays in Poynton, so I commuted for the entire summer, ensuring I returned in time to play for Poynton Cricket Club on Saturdays.

We finally moved from Poynton to Dunblane on 29 July 1981, the same day as Prince Charles married Lady Diana Spencer. To remember our Newmarket connection, Kate had brought an old horseshoe, which we affixed to the back door. We also changed the name from Capalt Burn back to its original name, The Arns.

I was now getting used to the daily return journey from Dunblane to Glasgow. The traffic volume increased as I neared Glasgow and became a slow progress for the last few miles on the M8 motorway. I had experienced holdups while working in Manchester, but a five-lane motorway into Glasgow with creeping traffic was something else. The Barclays Life office was on the first floor above the bank's branch at 90 St. Vincent Street. There were limited parking spaces around the back of the building, but a small bribe to Charlie, the parking attendant, usually secured a spot (otherwise, I had to park at a nearby fee-paying multistorey car park). I sometimes needed the car to visit appointments with the salespeople, so travelling by train was not always an option, despite the excellent rail network.

The 1981 Barclays Life Northern Regional Conference was to be held in Scotland for the very first time in March, instigated by Graham Kenward. We had an early meeting of the Northern regional managers at the prestigious Turnberry Hotel on the Ayrshire coast to assess the venue and discuss the programme. Bobby Charlton, the Manchester United footballer, was to be one of the guest speakers on the first afternoon. I was tasked with meeting him for lunch and was to function as his host. He was one of my favourite footballers; I had seen him play for England many times at Wembley, including the World Cup matches of 1966 when he scored some fantastic goals against Mexico and Portugal. I had also been at the 1968 European Cup final with my brother Dennis when Manchester United defeated Benfica 4–1 after extra time, to be the first English club to lift the trophy. Having been given this task, I could not wait for the conference and dug out the 1968 European Cup final programme I had kept ready for him to sign.

When the day came, I met him, and we firstly had lunch together, discussing the European Final of 1968 and the World Cup Final 1966, among other career highlights. He was one of the survivors of the Manchester United air crash of 1958, though I wasn't sure whether to mention this. However, he was quite happy to talk about it, and when asked if it made him nervous of flying, he said, "Not really, considering the number of flights that take place every day, and not when you consider that when travelling by rail, the wheels could easily come off the narrow track." He was quite easy to converse with. When he signed my programme, he said, "You don't see many of these, these days." I introduced him at the conference, mentioning his career highlights after a short film of the 1968 European Cup final, which he had brought with him. During his presentation, he spoke about having belief in what you do in life, which was very well received. He attended the evening gala dinner, and features in the photograph of my Barclays Life Scotland team which hangs on my study wall to this day.

I had become a member of the LIA whilst in Manchester, and attended the monthly meetings in Glasgow, held at the Central Station Hotel in the evenings. The meetings were well attended by salespeople and managers, so I soon became friendly with many of the other managers who attended from the various Life companies. It was during one of these meetings that the decision was taken to form a managers' forum, so that the managers could meet by themselves and exchange ideas. Two years later, I became the chairperson. This entitled me to attend the National LIA Managers' Forum Conference. I felt it important to stay connected with what was happening nationally in the industry and locally, as Barclays Life salespeople in Scotland had no bank liaison to help them meet sales targets. Any ideas that I could glean from others was going to be key to making Barclays Life Scotland a success.

My strategies worked; so well that Barclays Life management decided to open an office in Aberdeen, now there were enough numbers to warrant the cost. This took place on 31 August 1981 with much publicity in the local press. This prompted a title change in January 1982 when I became Manager Scotland (rather than District Manager Scotland). The title change had no monetary benefit although I was now managing two districts: Aberdeen and Glasgow. The drawback to this new arrangement was that management wanted to move the manager they had in Newcastle, John Waterworth, to Aberdeen, under my supervision. John was married with a family and lived in North Shields. I had met his family one evening previously following attendance at a Newcastle branch meeting whilst working as RMA with Graham Kenward. I had got to know John well. He had a dependency on alcohol but had been successful as a salesperson prior to becoming the Newcastle manager, so there was obviously something he had to offer. Before he started as manager for Aberdeen, I invited him to dinner one evening at the Dunblane Hydro Hotel. I asked Kate to join us, keen to gain her female perspective. I laid out the strategy for the development I had for Scotland as a whole, with reference to his role as the manager of Aberdeen. Kate had noticed that he seemed nervous and went along with all my ideas without offering any input.

A few weeks after he commenced the role, I was asked to meet Tony Henden, director of Barclays Life, at Glasgow Airport one morning. He had flown up from London for an onward flight to Aberdeen, on which we were both booked. It was a tiny aircraft with no more than 10 passengers. I remember the flight well as it had been snowing several days previously all over Scotland. The plane flew at no more than 10,000ft; there were fantastic views of the countryside all the way. I was told that the purpose of Tony's visit was not to be broadcast – upon meeting him at Glasgow, I learned that he wanted to prove that John Waterworth had an alcohol problem. (As a member of bank staff, they had an obligation to try to help him.) We landed at Aberdeen Airport and took a taxi to the office in Aberdeen, arriving just before 9am. By 11am, John had still not arrived. He came soon after and had obviously been drinking. Tony Henden discussed his problem with him and stated that he was to be suspended immediately, with the choice of seeking help or being dismissed. With John's suspension, I was once again in charge of the whole of Scotland. I mention this episode because it had a bearing on my decision to later leave Barclays Life.

In early 1982, Jenny Perris retired, so I had to recruit another secretary. Following interviews with several potential candidates, I choose Irene Aitken. Irene was married but had no other family. She lived in Giffnock, just outside Glasgow centre, and proved to be very capable.

Barclays Life had only ever held an annual national sales conference in England, but, in 1982, they decided to hold a qualifying conference in Jersey in the Channel Islands. The targets were sales-based for managers and salespeople. Along with eight of my salespeople, I qualified. The invitation included Kate and our three children and was held at the luxurious Grand Hotel in St. Helier, the capital of Jersey. It was a fantastic three days; in between the business parts of the conference, there were many relaxation events from which to choose. One of the options was to have a courtesy hire car for the day. We opted for this so we could visit Gorey Bay, and the Gorey Hotel where we had spent our honeymoon 18 years previously, which we wanted to show the children. It was a poignant moment as we stopped off in Gorey Bay, the first time Kate and I had been back since 1964. We found the Gorey Bay Hotel where we had spent our first seven days as Mr and Mrs Nash.

The after-dinner speaker on the Friday evening was Henry Cooper, later knighted to become Sir Henry Cooper. Cooper was a heavyweight boxer who narrowly missed defeating Cassius Clay (Mohammed Ali) to win the World Heavyweight Championship in 1966. For the gala dinner on the Saturday evening, Fred Trueman the cricketer was the after-dinner speaker, who, at the time, held the Test match record of taking the most wickets (307). I still have the dinner menus signed by both men.

Following the success of this 'overseas' conference, the following year, Barclays Life announced another conference, this time to be held on the island of Malta. Again, it was sales-based for salespeople and managers, but harder to achieve. When the results were announced, I was confident that I had done enough to warrant qualification. However, I did not appear on the final list. I challenged John Hibell who had now taken over as national sales manager. It became apparent that the sales figures for Aberdeen had not been counted in my overall total. This news astonished me as John Waterworth had only been manager for a short time before I had taken overall responsibility again. I pointed this out, but to no avail – he would not change his mind. This came as no real surprise as he had notified the Northern area managers at an earlier meeting that managers' meetings and overnight stays were to cease to save costs. Barclays Life would save even more by not inviting me to the Maltese conference.

Earlier in the year, there had been several management changes, caused by Peter Horrocks, the national sales manager, leaving the company. John Hibell had been promoted to the role after formerly being the Midlands regional manager. Graham Kenward, my boss and Northern region manager, had also left to become the national direct sales manager for Target Life. Tony Hodgson had now been promoted to Northern Regional Manager from his position as manager of Manchester; Bill Jacklin, the Liverpool manager, had moved across the M62 to become the Manchester manager. Had I still been RMA and not taken the Scotland manager's job, I could have been the new branch manager for Manchester.

Meanwhile, Tony Hodgson was now my new boss. He made the decision to hold the next Northern regional conference in Scarborough. This came as no surprise as Tony had his origins in Hull. He organised a managers' meeting at the Scarborough Hotel to assess the venue's suitability. The two-day meeting followed the normal format, during which I received a phone call to say that two Barclays Bank inspectors would be coming to interview me over car expense claims. I could not think to what they were referring. I soon learned during the interview: they wanted an explanation as to why I had authorised new tyres on my Morris Ital just before its compulsory 40,000 miles, at which point the car would be changed. They also wanted me to explain why the headlamps had been replaced. I found it amazing that two Barclays Bank employees had been deployed to Scarborough to interview me about such insignificant matters when I could have given an explanation over the phone. I politely told them, without losing my cool, that it was illegal to drive with worn tyres below the statutory tread depth, and that without proper headlights, I could not see in the dark. (I was travelling regularly up and down the A74 from Scotland to England, a dangerous road before it became a motorway in the 1990s.)

Barclays were querying these essential costs, yet two people had driven to Scarborough and had an overnight stay just to have a 30-minute chat about it.

Soon after returning from this meeting, I took a phone call one evening at home from Graham Kenward. He asked me to meet him for a chat – he wanted to discuss the opportunity of the Glasgow branch manager's job for Target Life. Graham had been at Target Life for about three months, responsible for building up the direct salesforce. I agreed to meet and drove down to the village where he lived – Harpenden, just outside London. He had arranged to chat over dinner at a restaurant called Gleneagles. He had also invited Mike Fuller who I had known when he was employed as an actuary for Barclays Life but who had recently joined Target Life. They outlined the opportunity for branch managers and the vision the directors, John Stone and Paul Taylor, had for Target Life: to make the company successful so it could be floated on the stock market. At that time, the company was partly owned by Jacob Rothschild of the famous Rothschild dynasty. If I agreed, I would be on a first-year, guaranteed salary of £30,000, plus car, pension and private healthcare. (My Barclays Life salary was £10,663.) I had no knowledge of Target Life or how successful the company was, nor indeed the success record of John Stone and Paul Taylor. However, the opportunity and package being offered was mind-blowing. I remember asking what happened if I failed. Mike Fuller was the first to reply:

"Mick, if you fail, we all fail."

I informed them that I would need to discuss all the details with my wife, which they understood, so I returned to Dunblane the next day.

Kate had not heard of Target Life. I relayed the details, and she was sceptical, so when Graham Kenward telephoned, I said we had yet to make a firm decision. He then offered to come up to Dunblane to answer any further questions we had. We agreed. He asked me to book dinner at the five-star Scotland Gleneagles Hotel, just up the road from The Arns. After dinner, we returned to The Arns where he was staying overnight. We discussed the job offer into the early hours over brandy and coffee.

The next day, we came to a decision. It became termed 'The Gleneagles Agreement'. I was aggrieved at the way I had been treated by Barclays Life: not being invited to the Maltese conference and the petty way I had been grilled by the bank's inspectors over my car expenses. I had received good appraisals for my job as manager of Scotland; had built up a good sales team and increased the sales of Barclays Life policies. If that was the way I was to be treated for being successful, then I would resign. I addressed my resignation to Tony Hodgson, the Northern regional manager. Tony Hodgson, though a very capable person, in my view was not strong enough for the regional manager's position, and so it proved. A year later, he left after being offered the job of National Sales Manager for Refuge Assurance. He later succeeded in recruiting my previous manager from Peterborough, Ted Green, a decision Ted admitted years later was a big mistake on his part.

With the decision made and resignation submitted, I then had to break the news to my sales team. Irene, my secretary, was disappointed, having only just settled into her role, but she understood that if I saw the move as an opportunity, I should take it. I called a branch meeting, asking her to book a room at the hotel beside Glasgow Queen Street station (now the Millennium Hotel). It was one of the worst things I have had to do: break the news to my supportive and loyal team. Not only were they a good group of work colleagues, but they had also helped my family and I to settle in Scotland. I decided that I would open the meeting but then hand it over to Bob Pringle, the senior group controller. I told them I would be leaving and then left the meeting. I went straight home, unable to comprehend what I had done. I knew there would be disappointments. However, I have never been one to turn down opportunities, not wanting to ever look back and wonder what if.

Kate and I decided to host a leaving party as a thank-you. It was held at The Arns on 26 February to which everyone was invited, including Jenny, my previous secretary. Everyone came, and I was presented with a beautiful chess set. This has been used many times and reminds me of what a great team we were over the course of those three years.

I do not think my resignation came as a surprise to Tony Hodgson who made no attempt to talk me out of it. I served a month's notice and did not attend any more managers' meetings.

Having had all the security of a manager with the Barclays Bank Group, it would now be a different scenario. Despite the salary and benefits offered by Target Life, we no longer had the benefit of a Barclays low-cost mortgage and other staff privileges. So, the first task was to seek out a new mortgage deal for The Arns from another provider.

11

TARGET LIFE

I received my new branch manager's contract, starting on 1 March 1983, with a guaranteed first year's salary of £30,000, plus a company car, non-contributory pension scheme, private health care, permanent health insurance, and life cover. After the first year, I would be paid a salary of £15,000, plus quarterly bonuses, dependent on branch profitability. Target Life had pioneered a profit centre concept for branch managers which meant the more profitable your branch, the more you earned.

My priority was to choose a new company car. I was recommended a Rover, the choice of the other managers, so I went along to the Dunblane Motor Company, a local garage, to order one.

I had to attend an induction course at Target's head office in Aylesbury, Buckinghamshire. I drove down from Scotland and located the offices, checking in at reception upon my arrival. I was directed to a building on the other side of reception and told to take the lift, where someone would meet me. As the lift door opened, a hand offered to shake mine, and I heard the words, "Welcome, my name's Roger Kelting." I was taken up to the top floor where the training room, board room and accommodation were situated. I was shown to the training room, within which were other new personnel – from Wales, Sheffield and Oxford – already waiting to attend the same induction course as me. Graham Kenward had been instrumental in recruiting managers from across the country. However, we were not staying in this building – we had been booked in at a local hotel – and I would be sharing with a chap from Sheffield, called Noel White.

The induction meeting was run by the training manager George Stride, an industry legend for training salespeople in the Life Insurance business and who had also written several books on the subject. We were introduced to Ben Allen, assistant to Graham Kenward, before then introducing ourselves. During the week, we learnt about the company's background. Founded in the early 1960s, Target Life had been transformed after Charterhouse J. Rothschild bought it in 1980. John Stone became managing director in 1981 and began developing Target to be an upmarket life insurance company. The Target Life products were to be a big part of this vision. The first was a life product marketed for all ages, called Masterplan. Principally a lifelong plan, though it could be taken out for certain periods of a person's life, it was structured over 25 years. They also had the Maximum Investment Plan. The Target Life Pension Plan was a popular product and a market leader, performance-wise, something Barclays Life did not have until much later. The charges on the pension plan were based on 'initial' and 'accumulation' units, something I had not encountered before. During the first two years, initial units would be allocated to the plan but would always be subject to a 3.5% charge. Thereafter, the monthly premiums would be allocated to the accumulation units and subject to a 0.5% charge. This was known as 'front loading'.

Their products attracted good commissions which was how they were paid for – a very clever marketing concept. We were also introduced to a new savings plan that was about to be launched: the Gold Plan. This was a 25-year savings plan that could be cashed in after 10 years. The monthly premiums were invested in gold stocks and gold mining. Gold was an attractive investment at the time, despite the UK having dropped the gold standard several years earlier as a measure of the country's wealth. I can remember the days when we lived in Newmarket, and gold bullion used to be transported through the town in the early hours on its way to Mildenhall US Airforce base for loading onto a cargo plane bound for the USA and Fort Knox. For security reasons, we only knew about it after the event.

After each day of the course, we were wined and dined at The Bell Hotel at Aston Clinton, where, on the first night, John Stone and Paul Taylor joined us for dinner. No expense was spared. Retiring to our hotel to sleep, I had some difficulty as my roommate was a habitual snorer, which he had warned me about. I somehow got through the week and came back to Scotland highly motivated and confident I had made the right choice in leaving Barclays Life.

My Target Life direct sales office was in Glasgow at Charing Cross, just off the M8 motorway. I was on the same floor as the Target Life main broker division whose manager was Charlie Carpenter. Also on the same floor was the Target Life specialist division, managed by a lady whose first name was Penny. The main broker division supported independent brokers who sold Target policies, as well as other companies, whilst the specialist broker division looked after specialist brokers that sold large Target investment bonds and corporate pensions.

I had inherited the secretary, Shirley Frew, from Joe Capaldi who was the previous direct sales manager. I knew of Joe Capaldi from Million Dollar Round Table (MDRT) (more on that later) but had never met him. The secretaries of each division shared an office on the same floor. I was made welcome on the first morning and learned from Shirley that I only had four salespeople – retaining and recruiting had been a problem.

The four personnel were: Andrew Grieve, who had been with Target Life several years and was in fact an employee; Keith Campbell, relatively new; Jimmy Higgins, who had just joined after leaving a career in teaching, and Danny Moran. Apart from Andrew, all the other salesmen were self-employed. Shirley gave me a summary of all four men, stating that I might find Andrew Grieve difficult to get on with as he was very set in his ways; he sold exclusively to doctors and surgeons and was prone to bouts of depression. His sales title was Senior Consultant, and he lived in East Kilbride. Keith Campbell was also a senior consultant and lived in Callander. He worked part-time hours as he had other outside interests, including studying part-time. Jimmy and Danny were consultants, both still trying to get themselves established. Armed with this information, I decided I would try to get to know them better and arranged for Shirley to invite them in during the week for a chat. I wanted to meet them and then take them to lunch at The Fountain, a restaurant opposite with an excellent reputation.

Andrew was the first of the four I met. He wasted no time in telling me that he did not like attending branch/sales meetings and preferred to work on his own. I said that I had no problem with that but that there would be occasions when he would need to attend, otherwise he could miss something important that might be of use to him. I asked him to explain how he got his sales as he was operating in a very exclusive market among doctors and surgeons. As he explained his way of working, I told him that I knew of the unique opportunity these people had to buy back years in pension benefits, as well as taking out a pension for their wives, if they helped with administration and provided a secretarial role. Upon hearing this, he became chattier, and I promised him a technical paper on the subject. Despite my earlier misgivings, we got on very well; so much so that without me asking, he gave me feedback on the other three salespeople.

Meeting the other three later, I realised that Andrew produced most of the business. Keith was doing an Open University course, for which not even he knew the purpose of, and Jimmy and Danny were cold calling telephone numbers in the evenings for appointments. I realised I needed to recruit some new blood, and fast!

After giving it some thought, I thought about my Barclays Life team, who, after all, had no bank liaison or leads to work with, but had the opportunity to earn much more commissions with Target than they would with Barclays Life. I therefore had no guilt in approaching anyone that I had recruited. Joining in the first couple of months were John Doherty and Pat Hyatt. Carmen Capaldi came after a year, followed by Mian Sadiq. In a short time, I had doubled the team members. I then received a telephone call from Eric Band who was Jean Band's brother. He had been posted to Barclays Bank in Glasgow following his marriage to a Scots girl. He said that his mother would be moving up to Scotland later in the year and that rather than be left behind in Bolton, his sister wondered whether she could leave Barclays Life in Manchester and join my team in Glasgow. I invited her for a chat, explaining how Target operated and the potential for higher earnings. She had no hesitation in wanting to join and began house hunting in readiness to move up to Scotland. I have always believed that people work for people, not companies or organisations. The same is true of sport: people play for people, not the clubs.

Each one of my new recruits had to attend technical training courses in Aylesbury at Target's head office, so they were qualified to market the Target Life products, after which they began as Associates, the starter grade.

It was towards the end of my first year when Graham Kenward persuaded John Stone to make some regional changes to Target Life's setup in Scotland. The change had come about due to the lease on an Edinburgh office expiring – a Target unit trust office shared with Target Life Edinburgh branch. The lease was not being renewed, and, in the interests of efficiency, it had been decided to amalgamate everything into the Glasgow office. Edinburgh also had a sub-branch in Aberdeen. Both were managed by Bill Grant, who also did part-time work, modelling clothes for catalogues and fashion magazines. David Black was his unit manager for the Aberdeen area, looking after a small team operating out of offices in Dee Street. In Graham's opinion, Bill Grant was not totally focused on developing Edinburgh or the Aberdeen area, so by closing the Edinburgh office, all the salespeople, including Bill Grant and those in Aberdeen, would now report to me in Glasgow. The Target Life sales teams would now be known as Scotland Branch. This obviously did not go down too well with Bill Grant who promptly resigned and went to work as the Edinburgh manager for Hill Samuel Life Assurance. I now had the responsibility of all the Target Life salespeople in Scotland, just as I had had with Barclays Life. Some of the people I inherited from this change were to become some of my best salespeople: John McMahon in Edinburgh, William Lane and Ken Mackie in Aberdeen.

Once the changes were announced, I had called meetings with both Edinburgh and Glasgow personnel to see everyone, aware that people are resistant to change, especially as I was very much a new boy to Target. I shared my strategy for developing Scotland and found no real objections. I came away from the initial meetings feeling incredibly pleased. In a short time, I now had as many salespeople as I had had with Barclays Life, plus another of my Barclays Life recruits, George Donald from Lossiemouth, who had also agreed to join the Aberdeen sub-branch.

All was going well, when, during the national sales meeting at Coventry in November, word got round that John Stone was calling all managers to a special meeting the next day to discuss some major changes. This meeting was being held on the second day at Coventry. Unbeknown to me, several of the longer-term branch managers had been in discussion about being able to offer products not available from the Target Life stable. These included general insurance, private healthcare, and other insurance products. This had appealed to John Stone, as the theory was that if you offered clients a complete service for all their insurance needs, it would prevent them going elsewhere.

It also meant there was less chance of clients having their policies re-brokered, an industry problem at that time.

The meeting was very productive. John Stone, shrewd person that he was, saw the opportunity to make each branch manager exclusively responsible for running his own branch and associated costs. In return, the manager would be paid all the gross commissions into his branch account and be responsible for paying out the commissions to his salespeople, as well as office rent, secretaries' salaries and benefits, telephones, and all costs associated with running the office. Should the manager wish to advance anyone money for policies sold but not yet on risk, then, again, that would be his responsibility. A large amount of money was being sanctioned every month for this purpose by the directors of Target Life, so they would be pleased to get rid of this burden. Being new to the company, I was not certain how this would all work, but when discussing it with some of the more established managers, I could see the opportunity. It would, however, require careful budgeting, especially control of costs. We all went away from the meeting incredibly positive, and on my drive back to Scotland I stopped off at a phone box to call the office. My secretary, Shirley, had already heard on the grapevine about the changes. She was very irate and wanted to know if she still had a job. I told her that she would be briefed when I returned to the office.

On 1 January 1984, Target Financial Consultants came into being as a subsidiary of Target Life Assurance Company Limited. Graham Kenward was no longer sales director; Ben Allen had been elevated to the position of Development Director. The branch managers were asked to sign new contracts which included a clause guaranteeing renewal commission on all policies after five years' service that would accrue as a 'buyout' upon leaving or retirement. I had to negotiate a year's grace of not being charged for the rent on the Glasgow office until I found a new location with much more affordable rent. The system was set up – all I had to do now was make it work. John Stone was keen to make branch managers feel they had ownership of the company, so a meeting was convened at the Institute of Directors in London to personally receive from Jacob Rothschild a gift of 500 shares in Target Financial Consultants.

It was early February 1984 when Ken Mackie from the Aberdeen office called me one evening at home to complain that David Black, the Aberdeen unit manager, was not fulfilling his role. He only appeared in the office twice a week, sometimes less, and was more concerned with selling Mira showers than looking after the salespeople. He was effectively taking a 10% override for doing nothing. I made the decision to assess the situation by finding out when he was next expected in the office. Staying overnight in Aberdeen, I was in the office at 9am the following morning. David Black eventually appeared around midday. I confronted him and asked him for an explanation, but he became very confrontational, so I informed him that he had 15 minutes to collect his things as he was no longer required.

He said, "And if I don't?"

"As an employee of Target Life, I will call the police to have you removed from company property."

He very quickly departed, and the remaining salespeople were pleased to see the back of him. In mid-February, Ken Mackie was appointed the new unit manager.

The big breakthrough came with the threat of Life Insurance Premium Relief (LAPR) being withdrawn by the government in the 1984 budget. Premiums paid into 'qualifying life policies' attracted 15% tax relief prior to 14 March 1984. This in effect meant that a £10 per month policy only cost £8.50. In true salesmanship style, my salespeople were encouraged to show the 15% relief as a bonus. This meant the client could have a policy for £11.76 that only cost them the £10 net, the difference being contributed by the government. Plus, the policyholder got higher life cover for the extra 15%. As the deadline approached, everyone was focussed on contacting as many existing policyholders as they could, encouraging them to top up their existing life cover, as well as contacting prospects who had shown an interest but not yet purchased anything. This was, as we marketed it, 'the last chance opportunity to get something from the government'. The acceptance was overwhelming; applications were being written right up to the midnight deadline of 14 March 1984. I had arranged for the salespeople to deliver the last batch to my home so that a courier could deliver them to Target's head office before the clock struck midnight.

The following month, once all the applications were processed and put on risk, I received my branch account statement. It showed a credit of over £8,000. Once I had paid the salespeople their percentage, according to grade, I had a decent balance to carry forward.

Knowing I had to change premises, I began to look for something nearer to Dunblane to avoid the daily tortuous return journey into Glasgow. It was Keith Campbell who notified me of some offices in Stirling that were being converted from the John Player building, the former management offices for the John Player factory. John Player was a major cigarette producer, and in 1965 launched Players No. 6 which was to be the number one brand until the mid-1970s, when the dangers of nicotine were becoming apparent. In 1978, the factory closed. The site lay derelict, until it was gifted by John Player to Stirling to develop an industrial park for small startups. I arranged to meet up with the director, Derek Gavin, who had been appointed by the trustees to view the premises. No one had yet taken any of the units due to be constructed within the building. He showed me around the old factory. It had a ghostly feel; everything left from the final day of production. There was a strong smell of tobacco everywhere and some tobacco leaves were still hanging up where they'd been dried. We moved on to what had been the management offices. Here, work had just started – converting a first floor, open plan office into individual units. He informed me that the trustees' brief was to offer the units to startup companies – he was not sure whether Target Financial Consultants would qualify. However, as he was having difficulty attracting interest, the presence of a company that was part of the Target Life Group might attract others. It would be another two months before the first-floor offices would be ready to occupy, but, in the meantime, he could offer us temporary offices for a reduced rate in what had been the directors' offices of John Player on the ground floor. The suggestion was ideal; I could not wait to move away from Glasgow.

I broke the news to Shirley, my secretary, telling her I had found a suitable location. Provided it met with the approval of the Target property department, we would be moving to Stirling. She decided that it was too far for her to commute so would be leaving. I was not too disappointed, as, though capable, she was not ideal, and was a smoker, something I was not keen on. So began my search for a new secretary. We moved everything to Stirling in the summer of 1985, and until I recruited a replacement for Shirley, Kate became my temporary secretary and did a great job of keeping the office functioning.

I finally succeeded in recruiting a new secretary from the local job centre where I had advertised the position. Linda Moodie was my appointment, married to a local police officer. Linda had been married previously and had a son who was eight years old. Linda was a model secretary – fast typist and took shorthand.

Having established the premises, the priority was now recruiting more salespeople.

A further development took place in June 1984 when Jacob Rothschild Group sold Target Life to Morgan Grenfell, institutional investors, with Target staff taking a 12% stake. My 500 shares were now worth £60 a share. The deal for managers, however, was that 50% had to be invested in the new company – Target Group PLC – the remainder would be a loan note of £15,000. Some of my salespeople also invested personal funds, which was encouraging.

The following year, between January and March, there was further frenzied activity as rumours had circulated that the then chancellor, Nigel Lawson, would withdraw tax relief on pension contributions in his March budget. Pension sales boomed, with advertising both nationally and locally, but in the event the tax relief remained. Recruitment of further salespeople took a back seat during this time but soon picked up again. I received a congratulatory letter from Ben Allen in his capacity now as sales director for achieving the validation target.

In 1986, Target launched the Residential Property Fund, available to lump sum investors and monthly savings. This boosted sales and was particularly popular at the first ever Glasgow Money Show where we had a stand.

The Target Group was being prepared for flotation on the stock market, but in August 1987, it became headline news in the financial services and life industry when TSB banking group decided to make a bid for £220m. TSB paid £4.11p a share for the privilege – my 50% investment from the Rothschild buyout had now really done well. John Stone and Paul Taylor's goal had been achieved: Target Group was now a public company. To ensure that the existing management structure remained, TSB offered cash incentives to branch managers. For salespeople, a national sales incentive was launched, with John Humphreys from BBC Radio 4 presenting it at the National Sales Conference in Birmingham, cars being the main prizes in each category of salesperson.

Mian Sadiq, one of my senior consultants, really went for the BMW car – the prize for his position. The sales targets were high and demanding, but day after day he came in with new business, boosting his chances. The admin staff processed the applications, so by the time of the closing date we knew he had a good chance, though Leicester branch also had a senior consultant targeting the same prize. It was close right up until the last day, but Sadiq won, and I had the honour of going to the BMW garage in Glasgow to be photographed handing him the keys to his brand-new car.

The Scotland branch manager's job now became more demanding due to the geographical coverage and the control of sales. In August 1988, the Financial Services Act came into being, with the Securities and Investment Board (SIB) bringing in controls to monitor mis-selling. Compliance now became a big issue; each product sold had to be accompanied by a 'Reason Why' document. To assist me, Ben Allen suggested I appoint an assistant branch manager, and Keith Campbell, Jean Band and Willie McVey (the latter I had recruited as pensions manager) applied. Ben flew up to Scotland to do the interviews and recommended Jean Band. So, Jean took on the sales monitoring, when not training, and functioned as my deputy when I was away at branch managers' meetings and other duties at Target House in Aylesbury. For me, this meant catching the early morning shuttle at around 6am out of Edinburgh Airport for the flight to Heathrow. British Airways had recognised the need for business travellers to turn up and board without prebooking, just like boarding a train or bus. One simply paid on board with cash or a credit card. BA boasted that if one of their flights was full, they would provide a backup shuttle. And they did – on one occasion, there were just six of us on the flight. On St. Andrew's Day, they would sometimes send up Concorde. Although not flying supersonic, it was a great moment if you were lucky enough to be on it. Ben Allen would always meet me at Heathrow upon landing and drive to the meeting locations.

Ben was the perfect sales director – very fair-minded and disciplined, which came from his army background. This was well demonstrated at the overseas national sales conferences. He would go a few days early to check out the location, so that when all the delegates arrived, everything ran like clockwork. One of his disciplines was the gala dinner. Each manager who qualified had to host a table of eight or ten people, depending on the number of representatives qualifying. A briefing was held in Ben's suite on the afternoon of the dinner, procedure and protocol explained. Dress would be very formal – dinner jackets and bow ties for the gentlemen and evening dresses for the ladies. Managers hosting the tables had to ensure that no gentleman removed his jacket or bow tie (no matter how warm it was) until after the formal speeches, and coffee had been served.

On 4 January 1988, John Stone decided to rebrand the direct sales products under a new name: National Financial Management Corporation. It was felt this would better reflect Target Financial Consultants' identity from the broker divisions. The products also had a distinct advantage in that they could be linked to other investment groups other than just the Target Group.

March 1989 saw the introduction of portable computers for the salespeople, which were being piloted by a small number (William Lane was the salesperson trialling PCs in Scotland.) The branch staff were now using electronic mail for contacting head office, with less telephone calls being made.

The sales team continued to grow; a sub-branch of Aberdeen was established in Inverness; more admin staff were required to process the new business. Firstly, came Marc Duff from a government youth employment scheme. Marc was local to Stirling and learned quickly. Madeleine Murray also came from a similar scheme and fitted in well with everyone. Maureen Nairns was the third administrator to be recruited, also from the government's scheme. New business was booming all over Scotland after making use of trade fairs and Highland shows. I had a touring caravan that was used as a trade stand, as well as for booking larger events at the Scottish Exhibition Centre and other locations. The main source came from inviting people to take part in a free prize draw, whereby they would fill in a form with their name, address and phone number, then tick which Target Life product they would like more information on. Most people choose something, so following up these leads and then obtaining referrals was the key to the sales success. So successful was this that I was named Branch Manager of the Year in 1988, beating all the branches in England. I was presented with an inscribed silver salver at the National Sales Conference.

Target Financial Consultants Scotland now had sub-branches in Edinburgh, Glasgow, Aberdeen and Inverness, and a total of 38 salespeople. Jean Band was appointed training manager to do the sales training inhouse. The branch was profitable, and a few of the salespeople were earning substantial commissions. Bristol and Leicester branches were also enjoying success. However, other branches around the country, though writing new business, were not as profitable due to managers not controlling their costs. I qualified, along with many of my salespeople, for national sales conferences in some exotic locations around the world: Cyprus, Egypt, New Orleans, The Bahamas, Dubrovnik, and Marrakech, and I was the host manager for a weekend in Paris. We stayed at the best hotels around the UK as Ben Allen believed success deserved the best. Managers' meetings were now held at Blenheim Palace, the birthplace and former home of Sir Winston Churchill. Overnight accommodation was at The Bear Hotel in the nearby village of Woodstock. (The Bear was one of the original coaching inns of old England.) Sir Peter Parker, chairman of British Rail, had now joined the Target Group as chair, with the specific purpose of helping the Target Group become a PLC, which had been the vision of John Stone and Paul Taylor. Sir Peter attended the evening dinners at The Bear Hotel as a special guest for the managers, following the day's business meeting at Blenheim Palace.

The annual managers' appraisal entailed meeting Ben at the honorary artillery club at Armory House in London where he was a member, over a superb lunch set within historic surroundings. Only managers who were making a success of their branch were invited;

others had to be content with their appraisal in his office at Bedford Square.

Ben would visit Scotland every two months and usually stay with us at The Arns. He would take Kate and I out to dinner the evening before at Gleneagles or Auchterarder House. His presence at my branch meetings was welcomed by everyone, and, if I needed him to fly up to help with interviews, he was always willing. On one occasion, he boarded the BA Glasgow shuttle instead of Edinburgh. I was left wondering where he was until I phoned into the office to learn of his mistake – he had also phoned in asking where I was! I didn't realise it at the time, but looking back on this incident, it may have been the possible early warning signs of dementia, a disease to which he eventually succumbed. He left on 30 March 1990 (either taking early retirement or was retired). He had been with Target for 17 years and sales director for the last five. I had seen this coming during the last two years, as some managers who were unable to run their profit centre, became disgruntled and complained about his methods to John Stone and Paul Taylor. There was a move to try to set the managers up as a board to replace him, of which I would have no part.

A dinner was held to say farewell in June, but I was away at an MDRT meeting so unfortunately did not attend. Whilst at this meeting, I took a telephone call from Linda Moodie who had decided to resign her position as branch administrator having been offered a job locally as a PA to a manging director, a job she had always craved.

Ben's replacement was Paul Wrightson, who immediately wanted to brush away the idea of managers operating as profit centres. His vision was the direct salesforce setup which had been pioneered by Mark Weinberg in the 1970s when he started Hambro Life; a success for 20 years but no longer the way forward for direct salesforces in the life insurance industry of the 1990s. I was asked to be a main platform speaker at his first national sales conference held in Bournemouth on 13 and 14 November 1990. My topic was 'In pursuit of excellence'. The previous evening, he had organised dinner with the managers, and the legendry Liverpool footballer Emlyn Hughes, AKA 'Crazy Horse', was the guest. The event was a big success and my speech, which related to MDRT, was well received.

I sensed changes were coming and a short time later I was summoned down to London for a chat. David Pine from Bristol and Jeremy Stuart-Cox from Leicester were also summoned. We were given times of 10am, 11am, and 12pm respectively. Scotland, Bristol and Leicester were the most profitable branches, and we sensed changes were coming as no other managers had been called. We arranged to meet afterwards to discuss the content of the meetings. Paul Wrightson had stated to all three of us that the profit centre concept was to cease, and that we had the choice of joining his new sales operation or becoming directly authorised as brokers. (Talk about throwing the baby out with the bathwater!) He made it clear that our salespeople would also be given the choice, and he would be holding presentations in each area to brief them. All three of us were astounded at this news. One thing of which he was unaware was that we all had contracts with vested rights in the policy renewals commission after five years' service. Would Target Group really be prepared to pay for all this?

Wrightson arranged the Scottish meeting at the Hilton Hotel in Glasgow one midweek evening and each of my salespeople got a personal invite to attend. Bob Bullivant came with him to add support. (Bullivant was the national sales manager for the specialist broker division and had never really understood direct sales.) I went along to listen as Wrightson outlined his ambition for an elite salesforce to be known as Personal Financial Planning (PFP). His argument was that if I set up as an IFA, I could not provide the security for them that he could. He was very persuasive in his argument.

A few days later, I called a team meeting at the Moodiesburn Hotel, just outside Glasgow, to give my team the opportunity to absorb what they had heard and to ask questions. There was a mixed response; I knew I had to act quickly to prevent everyone joining Wrightson's new PFP setup. I decided to set up my own limited company as a tied agent of Target Life. I applied to Companies House and registered Financial Planning Scotland Limited on 15 March 1991. Now I had to persuade my salespeople to stay with me and not migrate to Personal Financial Planning, the name of the new Target Life direct salesforce selling the same products but branded PFP. This was important, as if everyone left, it would mean I would lose the override on renewal commission that I had worked so hard to achieve. Jean Band, John Doherty, George Donald, William Lane and George McGillivray all decided to become consultants for Financial Planning Scotland. Disappointingly, Andrew Grieve, Lydia Brown, Carmen Capaldi and Mian Sadiq did not. However, after six months, Andrew and Lydia applied to come back as they could not stand the new PFP setup. I agreed to take them back, but they never received any shares in Financial Planning Scotland which I had given to those who had remained.

I now had to take stock and decide the future, as well as spend time ensuring my vesting rights, as a former Target Life branch manager, were paid.

12

FINANCIAL PLANNING SCOTLAND LTD

I registered Financial Planning Scotland (FPS) as a private limited company on 12 March 1991, appointing Jean Band as company secretary. At the same time, I applied for FPS to become a tied agent of Target Life/National Financial to have the continuity of selling the same financial products that everyone had been used to.

Whilst all this was taking place, it became very unsettling for the sales team, particularly as new business had to be processed through the Personal Financial Planning (PFP) division until FPS had the correct authorisation. I was also having to draw up new contracts for the salespeople so that they were appointed representatives of FPS. It was a very hectic time, having to think about all the legal requirements, new stationery, business cards, and opening bank accounts, whilst also arranging meetings.

One such meeting I organised was with Paul Taylor to discuss the vesting rights as a former Target branch manager now that I had left. The meeting took place at Target House in Aylesbury, Bob Bullivant also present. He began by bluntly asking what I wanted. His attitude made me realise this was not going to be a very amicable meeting, so I immediately decided to make my purpose abundantly clear. I stated that my branch manager's contract entitled me to vesting rights after five years and I wanted to know when this would be paid. Paul Taylor said that he would need to check with the legal department whether this was correct and would get back to me in due course.

On the flight back to Scotland I realised that difficult times were ahead if I was going to receive my entitlement. It was, after all, one of the main reasons I had left Barclays Life to join Target Life in March 1984. I telephoned David Pine, the Bristol branch manager, who had taken the same steps as me by forming his own company. We agreed to keep each other notified on any developments, but in the meantime would seek legal advice should there be no progress.

Suddenly, everything changed when it was announced that the TSB group were looking for a buyer for Target Life. (Things had not worked out as expected with the £220m price tag TSB paid when they purchased Target.) Eventually, an established life insurance company, Equity and Law, became the new owners of Target Life for the modest sum of £50m. Established since 1844, Equity and Law had been a traditional life office, where annual bonuses were added to a life policy as determined by the company's profits, but now saw an opportunity to recruit a direct salesforce selling unit linked policies.

Uncertainty circulated, until it was announced that the Target Life products would disappear from the market and be replaced by products from Equity and Law. A whole raft of training now had to take place, with everyone having to take exams to understand Equity and Law's products before being allowed to market them to the public. FPS now had to apply to become authorised as an appointed representative of Equity and Law.

It was whilst all this was taking place that my vesting rights from Target had been put on hold. I saw an opportunity to rekindle this when the annual general meeting of the TSB group was announced. It was to be held in Glasgow. I was a shareholder, having bought TSB shares during the floatation a few years earlier, and decided to attend. After the main agenda had been covered, there was an opportunity for the shareholding public to ask the board of directors questions. I patiently waited for my turn at the microphone, and, when it came, I asked, "Following the sale of the Target Life group to Equity and Law, what provision has been made in the accounts for buying out the vesting rights of the former Target Life direct sales branch managers?" There was a stunned silence as the chair of the meeting looked to his right and then to his left for someone to answer my question. The assembled public, which numbered several hundred, all looked in my direction as the silence continued. Eventually the chairman, realising no one else knew the answer, replied:

"We will make a note and look into it."

I had made my point in front of the board and several hundred shareholders. Whether this incident helped is uncertain, but it led to a lot of correspondence between my solicitor, George Pollock, Target Life, and Equity and Law's legal teams. On one occasion, George Pollock and I flew down from Scotland to meet with David Pine and his solicitor to compare notes at a service station on the M25. It all proved worthwhile as the entitlement to vesting rights was eventually confirmed. They would be paid over a period of four years, provided FPS remained a tied agent of Equity and Law. Over this period, I received the value of the vesting rights which I shared with my sales team, who had remained loyal, on the same basis and formula that I had agreed with Equity and Law.

Having lost some of my team, I decided to manage a smaller team and recruited Matt Neilson and Eddie Pollock who were struggling to make a go of it on their own with other companies. The advantage for them was that they were able to service the existing clients we had accumulated whilst being a branch of Target Life. Eddie Pollock also brought with him mortgage experience which I had decided to build up, promptly establishing Financial Planning Scotland Mortgage Division as a separate unit. With fewer people to manage, this would also allow me more time to advise and sell.

With everyone now trained on Equity and Law's products, opportunities arose to return to the existing client base to offer these previously unavailable products. Financial Scotland continued to feature as one of the top ten producers of new premium business. I qualified in my own right for a convention in Sun City, South Africa. This was my first experience of an overseas convention with Equity and Law, and it did not disappoint. A production bonus scheme had been introduced based on a percentage of the previous year's business. At Financial Planning Scotland, we succeeded in achieving this bonus year on year. Whilst this was all taking place, the previous Target managers who had moved to Equity and Law negotiated to have written into the principals' contract a five-year vesting right, like the previous one with Target Life.

Equity and Law was part of AXA Assurance, a French company, and on 24 August 1992, a decision was made to change the name to AXA Equity and Law. Once again, all the products had to be rebranded. This included all our company stationery and business cards, but, more importantly, my marketing tape packs. I had first seen this idea of an audio business card at an MDRT meeting. It consisted of a professionally produced audiotape with an introduction letter and business card. On the recording was an interview between me and a professional presenter, whereby I explained the benefit of pension planning. (I had paid a Radio Scotland presenter to do an interview with me after writing the script.) The finished product looked very professional and had led to many successful sales, so I was particularly keen to keep this going. I had financed the initial outlay, but I was now left with several unused packs that were no longer compliant due to the decision to change to AXA Equity and Law. I approached AXA with a request to help finance the rebranding but was rejected on the grounds that the budget had already been spent. For a company the size of AXA, this was peanuts, but it represented a significant cost to me. I sensed that there was more to this decision than the reason given but could not put my finger on it at the time.

In 1997, I decided to move the office's location from the John Player building in Stirling to my home address, The Arns in Dunblane. By this time, Andrew Grieve, Lydia Brown and John Doherty had all retired, Matt Neilson had emigrated to Japan, and William Lane had decided to pursue another line of business. This left only Jean Band and I, so cutting costs on office rents and rates was essential. Though this decision did not meet with AXA's approval, they reluctantly agreed to fund the cost of moving all the IT equipment to The Arns.

I also decided that I was no longer going to give advice on investments and pensions, instead advising on protection insurance, general insurance, and mortgages. Jean, therefore, would continue with the investment and pensions side but working with an IFA, not as an appointed representative of FPS. I had had enough of managing other people and looked forward to just being responsible for myself and the advice I would give. I applied to the Financial Services Authority for permissions for FPS to conduct advising and bringing about mortgage contracts and general insurance. After six weeks, permissions were granted, and FSA number 300952 was given to FPS on the register. I now had to take out professional indemnity insurance, make returns every six months to the FSA, and maintain continuing professional development. To do this, I attended meetings several times a year specifically arranged by mortgage and general insurance providers. Kate did the monthly accounts and bank reconciliations, and my eldest son, Graham, who was a qualified accountant, prepared the annual accounts for filing and corporation tax returns.

By now, most mortgage providers and insurance providers had online platforms that enabled applications to be input, and instant decisions given instead of the paper-based applications that could take days, sometimes weeks, to process. Every mortgage case, once completed, required building and contents insurance, plus life insurance for every borrower. Unlike my early days as a life insurance salesman in the 1970s, now many applications did not even require face-to-face meetings. Earning fees and commissions in the 21st century required far less travelling and was simpler (as long as you gave the correct advice and maintained meticulous records for inspection by the Financial Conduct Authority).

New business came by reputation; there was no need for advertising or marketing. I pride myself on having arranged mortgages for three generations of one family. There is also a residential area in Dunblane that has mortgages all arranged by me. Once I reached the age of 60, each time I tried to retire, the phone would ring, and someone would be having trouble getting a mortgage or required life insurance. Having always enjoyed being able to help people with their finances and solve their problems, with my experience it seemed a waste not to keep my company going. Finally, though, I decided at 75, after 44 years of offering advice, enough was enough. I notified the Financial Conduct Authority in January 2018 to withdraw my permissions on 31 March 2018. The last three months were hectic as, having heard that I was finally retiring, several people required mortgages and life insurance. It was on 2 April 2018 that FPS ceased being able to provide mortgage and insurance advice. The FCA could not commit to my date of 31 March as it was Eastertime, and their offices would be closed. So, on 2 April, their first working day back after the Easter break, they confirmed I was no longer authorised to practice.

There was quite a lot of pipeline business still to complete which was honoured both by mortgage lenders and insurers. FPS remained as a company until August 2020. After the loss of my dear wife Kate, who had replaced Jean Band as company secretary several years before, I decided to voluntarily strike FPS from the Companies House register. After 29 years and five months, I had signed off as a company director.

13

MDRT

I first learned of the Million Dollar Round Table (MDRT) when I was RMA for Barclays Life Northern region. MDRT, established in 1927, was based in the USA and was an elite organisation for those in the life insurance industry who had achieved above average sales success in a calendar year. Originally, the qualifying criteria was to sell $1m of life insurance cover within 12 months. However, this organisation was open to life insurance salespeople around the world who had sold an equivalent amount of life cover in their respective country. The qualification had to be approved by each Life office, verifying that the sales had been made. The individual also had to be a member of their country's recognised industry association – for the UK, this was the Life Insurance Association (LIA).

Whilst working for Barclays Life, I didn't know anyone who had qualified for MDRT though a lot of the salespeople were members of the LIA. I too joined the LIA whilst in Manchester and later became a Fellow, recognisable by years of service. It was when I moved to Target Life and attended local LIA meetings in Glasgow that I started to meet salespeople who were members of MDRT. At the time I was unable to qualify as I was a newly appointed manager for Target Life Scotland, and, since leaving Barclays Life, had done little personal selling. Target Life, however, encouraged their salespeople to qualify, with the added incentive of paying the airfare to attend the annual four-day MDRT conference held in the USA. People returned from these conferences saying how great they were and how wonderful the speakers. The attendees had listened and picked up new sales ideas.

In 1985, I persuaded my most successful adviser, William Lane, to attend the conference in New York. He had had a successful year and easily met the qualifying criteria. He returned, saying that the four days were very intense, but worthwhile. He had found it very motivational and learned a lot, not only from attending the main platform presentations, but the individual seminars held throughout the day.

Relying on his feedback, I decided to make the qualification for the 1986 meeting which was to be held in Orlando, Florida. 1986 was a family meeting which only took place every four years. I worked hard on my personal sales, as well as managing my sales team, and managed to qualify. With the venue being in Florida and a family affair to boot, I decided to take the opportunity to extend the trip and have a holiday after the meeting, taking Kate and Paul with me (the older children were now at university). We had recently purchased a timeshare apartment on the island of Guernsey, so we exchanged a week for one in Orlando. The flights and accommodation were all arranged, and we flew out of Prestwick Airport on Friday 27 June 1986. We arrived in Miami after a two-hour wait at New York Airport to change aircraft, where we later discovered Paul had left his denim jacket. I had booked a hire car from the airport for the drive from Miami to Orlando. The vehicle turned out to be an eight-seater station waggon. Paul happily sat in the rear seats, enjoying the drive to Orange Lake Country Club in Kissimmee, Orlando, where we had exchanged the timeshare week for a six-person apartment for two weeks. (There was a shortage in the pool of properties in the UK for people in the USA to come to at that time.)

The MDRT meeting started on the following Wednesday at the Orlando Conference Center. Firstly, I had to register as a new member, known as a provisional member. Once registered, I was required to attend a first-time member orientation meeting where I was briefed on the procedures, meeting format and etiquette. There were new members from all over the world, so it was a bit daunting at first, but the meeting hosts, who were all volunteers that had attended previously, were very friendly, providing suggestions on which main platform sessions and concurrent sales sessions to attend, according to an individual's needs.

On the morning of 29 June, we awoke early and drove to the Marriott Hotel in Orlando. Paul was to be left with all the other children whose parents were also attending the conference, to be looked after by specialist volunteers for the day. As we got out of the car, Gary, one of the host helpers, met us and ushered Paul on to a coach where other children had already boarded. Though he didn't know anyone, Paul went with the flow, and the last we saw of him he was sitting in a window seat as the coach drove off. It was only when he returned at the end of the day that we learned he had had a fantastic day at Disney World.

Kate and I went along to the Conference Center's meeting hall which was already filling to capacity. MDRT has an average of 15,000 international members, and though they do not all attend every year, it seemed as though many had arrived that day. We managed to find a couple of vacant seats with a view of the main platform and settled down in readiness to listen to the first speaker. As is customary, an invocation address was given by the president's wife before the other speakers began. Despite having retained the 1986 proceedings, I cannot remember which speakers we heard before the lunchbreak and which speakers we listened to for the next three days, but they were all highly motivational, especially for personal development and gaining transferable insurance sales ideas.

At the end of each day's proceedings, we met up with Paul for dinner after he had returned from his daily trips. He had been entertained all day, with further visits to the Epcot Center and SeaWorld, Florida's renowned theme parks. Four days after the MDRT meeting was over, we still had several days' holiday left, so we decided to see what Paul had experienced. It was completely mind-blowing, especially the fireworks display every night at the Epcot Center. Paul and I returned in October 1997 whilst Kate was doing an access course at Stirling University and visited all the theme parks once more – a fantastic father and son time.

Having been so impressed by the 1986 meeting in Orlando, I then qualified for later meetings in Chicago (1987), Atlanta (1988), Toronto (1989), San Francisco (1990), and Boston (1991). I was now a qualified member of MDRT and became a Life and Qualifying member in 1996 after 10 consecutive years of membership. This meant I did not need to submit production data to attend the annual meetings; rather, I maintained the life membership by paying the annual membership fee. This I did until 2000. By then, I had stopped attending the annual meetings, so the yearly fee of $500 no longer represented good value. Therefore, I allowed my membership to lapse.

Boston was the last meeting I attended, and, from this, a particular memory sticks in my mind. I left the hotel one morning and was walking to the Convention Center ready for the morning session, when I found the police had closed off the access. Not knowing the reason, I joined the crowd gathered up against the rope barrier, only to discover that they were waiting to see Senator Ted Kennedy who was campaigning to be elected senator of Massachusetts. As I couldn't get through, I waited for about half an hour, during which time I was given a banner to hold that simply read Kennedy. Shortly afterwards, Ted Kennedy came along, accompanied by his supporter, President Bill Clinton. Clinton shook hands with everyone at the front, and, as he reached me, I held out my hand. He shook it and thanked me for coming, assuming I was a local, holding as I did the banner in support of Kennedy.

The information and sales ideas I learned from these meetings were exceptional, one of which was the marketing audio tape packs mentioned previously. It also gave me the confidence to start my own company in March 1991, after AXA Equity and Law decided to abandon the branch profit centre concept.

I was one of the main platform speakers at the AXA Equity and Law sales conference in Bournemouth in 1990, having been asked by the sales director to speak about MDRT. I choose the title 'In Pursuit of Excellence' and for 20 minutes explained to the audience what MDRT had done for me and how valuable the organisation was for the life insurance industry. I concluded with suggesting everyone should aim to qualify for MDRT, at least once.

MDRT was a valuable part of my life. It gave me a lot more confidence and helped a great deal in my personal development, enabling me to manage my own company, as well as having a good work-life balance.

14

BARTERING COMPANY SCOTLAND

It was about two years after Ben Allen had retired from Target Life that I received a phone call from him. It was all rather mysterious – he said that there were two fellows who would be worth meeting for a chat if I was ever in London. He didn't give me any details other than to say they had an intriguing concept that may be of interest to me.

It was a short time later that I went to London to attend a cricket book club dinner prior to an England one-day international against Pakistan which was being held at Lord's the next day. As I would be staying overnight at the Baker Street Hotel where the dinner was being held, I arranged to meet the two men Ben had mentioned – Andrew Hennell and Jeremy Whittaker – in the afternoon. Andrew and Jeremy were the directors of The Baterting Company. The three of us met at around 3pm and I listened to their presentation on bartering. They had taken on a UK franchise with the concept of bartering goods and services and were looking to expand into Scotland. Bartering had formerly been used as a means of exchanging goods before the days of currency became the norm. The concept the two men put forward was to recruit companies, individuals, partnerships, and sole traders who would pay an annual joining fee to be able to deposit their goods or services into a bartering 'pool'. In return, they could then take out goods or services they required, of equal value. The only money to change hands would be the VAT element which still had to be accounted for to the Treasury.

I could not see immediately how FPS could benefit directly or indeed make use of our services in a bartering pool. We did, however, have a readymade sales team, so, on my flight home, I started to think about the possibility of how FPS could make use of a franchise in Scotland. I discussed this with some members of the sales team, who showed an interest. This resulted in Andrew and Jeremy being invited to make a presentation to everyone. After the presentation, it became clear that here was another opportunity for the salespeople to market financial services by using the bartering concept as an introduction. Due to the enthusiasm shown, I signed a franchise agreement with Andrew and Jeremy. The deal would provide 50% of sign-up fees and 50% of trade fees.

The established financial consultants soon began signing up companies, offering every type of goods and/or services that could be bartered. I took the decision to recruit more personnel as traders to facilitate the bartering pool. Advertisements were placed in national newspapers which attracted many applicants for interview. This in turn attracted TV and radio journalists who wanted to do interviews. So, I did a piece for Radio Scotland from the Stirling studios and a short TV clip was done for Grampian TV from The New Marcliffe Hotel in Aberdeen. (This was set up by siblings Richard and Lorraine Logie who lived in Aberdeen and had recently been recruited). We soon had trade consultants covering Scotland, offering numerous goods and services.

Once a firm or individual became a member, they were eligible to state what value of product or service they were placing in the 'pool'. They then confirmed what product or service they required in exchange for that value. It was then a question of signing up a firm or person that could meet that requirement. Bartering exchanges really took off; so much so that Lorraine Logie, who was a very switched-on individual, was appointed trade manager to oversee all the trades that were taking place. Seminars were arranged for firms and companies that had been signed up as members, and trade consultants' meetings were held regularly. Lorraine rented a flat in Stirling to be near the centre of activity and I took on the lease of another office at the John Player building to accommodate the extra personnel working as trade consultants. Maureen Nairns, an administrator for Financial Scotland, became The Bartering Company administrator. New computers with Windows software capability were purchased and extra telephone lines installed to cope with the volume of trades.

After 12 months of success, I decided to break away from The Bartering Company, which, as it transpired, was a franchise owned by an American named Buzz Remede. I wanted to do our own thing rather than give away half our revenue. I registered Bartering Company Scotland with Companies House as a separate entity in February 1992. This did not go down too well with The Bartering Company who tried to prevent us doing trades with the clients we had introduced, so we arranged for everyone to sign new agreements. In a short time, I found myself chairman of UK Bartering, as, by now, other companies had also been set up in England. Regular meetings were held in London at the Wig & Pen, an old ale house just across from the Royal Courts of Justice. This involvement increased when I attended a European bartering two-day seminar in Brussels and was surprised at the number of European companies offering bartering.

However, all was not well as the 'Logie factor', as we had termed Richard and Lorraine, was causing frustrations with them wanting a bigger share of control. They were offered the chance to buy into Bartering Company Scotland but did not accept that option. A considerable amount of money from the Target buyout had been used to get the bartering concept started, so I was not prepared to let them in for nothing. A meeting scheduled in Fort William, for which they did not turn up, was the first sign they were going their own way.

(Lorraine had already moved back to Aberdeen.) To replace her, we advertised in the Scottish national papers and recruited more people to facilitate the trades. The new people were trained on the concept, and all was set up when I left Jean Band in charge as co-director to take a holiday in South Africa in early January 1996. There, I watched the fifth and final Test match against South Africa. This series was the first since 1964–65 due to the apartheid years, so, being a cricket purist, it was significant after a break of 30 years.

Returning two weeks later after watching England get beaten in the fifth and final Test by 10 wickets and losing the series 1–0, I discovered that the newly recruited trade consultants were completely disillusioned with the whole concept of bartering. I called a meeting at a hotel in East Kilbride to try to discover what had demotivated them. There had been no supervision or backup whilst I was away, so I decided to wind down the concept rather than spend more time, energy and money building it back up again. Gradually trades and memberships ceased, resulting in Bartering Company Scotland being dissolved in January 1999. It had been an exciting concept and could have been even more successful, but I was now 56 and had been diverted away full-time from financial services for several years.

A recent check on the Companies House register revealed that Richard and Lorraine Logie set up The Business Exchange (Scotland) Limited in 1995. Richard is Managing Director, and the company is still active in bartering, though Lorraine resigned in 1997. I had recruited them, so it is pleasing to see that the concept remains a success.

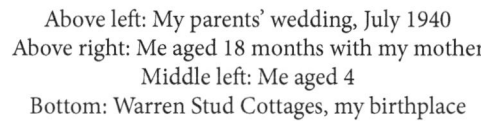

Above left: My parents' wedding, July 1940
Above right: Me aged 18 months with my mother
Middle left: Me aged 4
Bottom: Warren Stud Cottages, my birthplace

Above: My house at Great Barton, 1946-52
Middle right: A school photo of me with my
brother Dennis and sister Jill, 1955
Bottom: Cheveley C of E 1953/54 winning
Garden & Produce cups – I'm seated 4th
from left

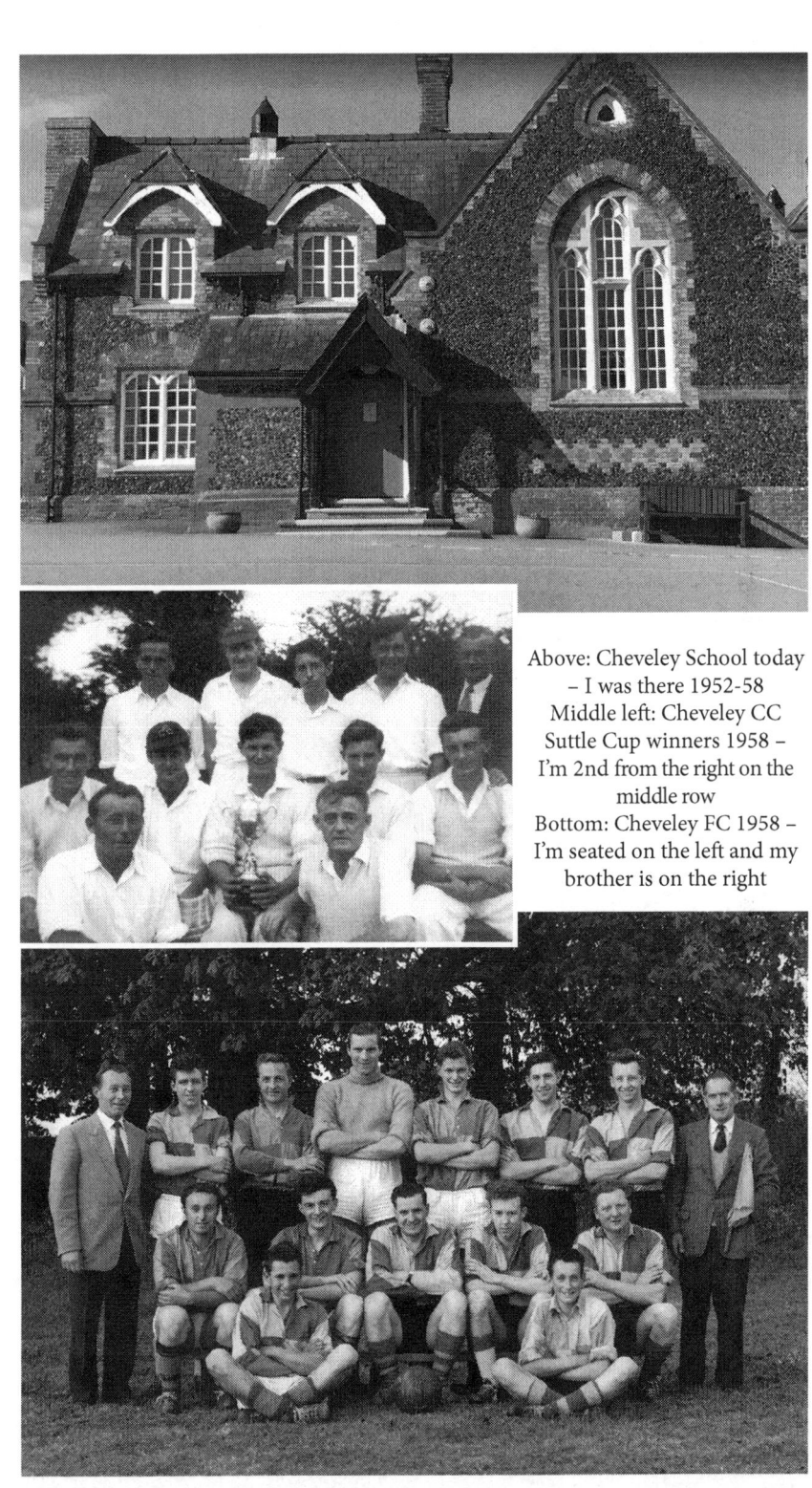

Above: Cheveley School today
– I was there 1952-58
Middle left: Cheveley CC
Suttle Cup winners 1958 –
I'm 2nd from the right on the
middle row
Bottom: Cheveley FC 1958 –
I'm seated on the left and my
brother is on the right

Above left: Our wedding day,
6 June 1964
Above right: Cutting the cake
Bottom main: Our honeymoon in Jersey
Botton inset: Our first home at 12 Heathbell
Road, Newmarket, September 1964

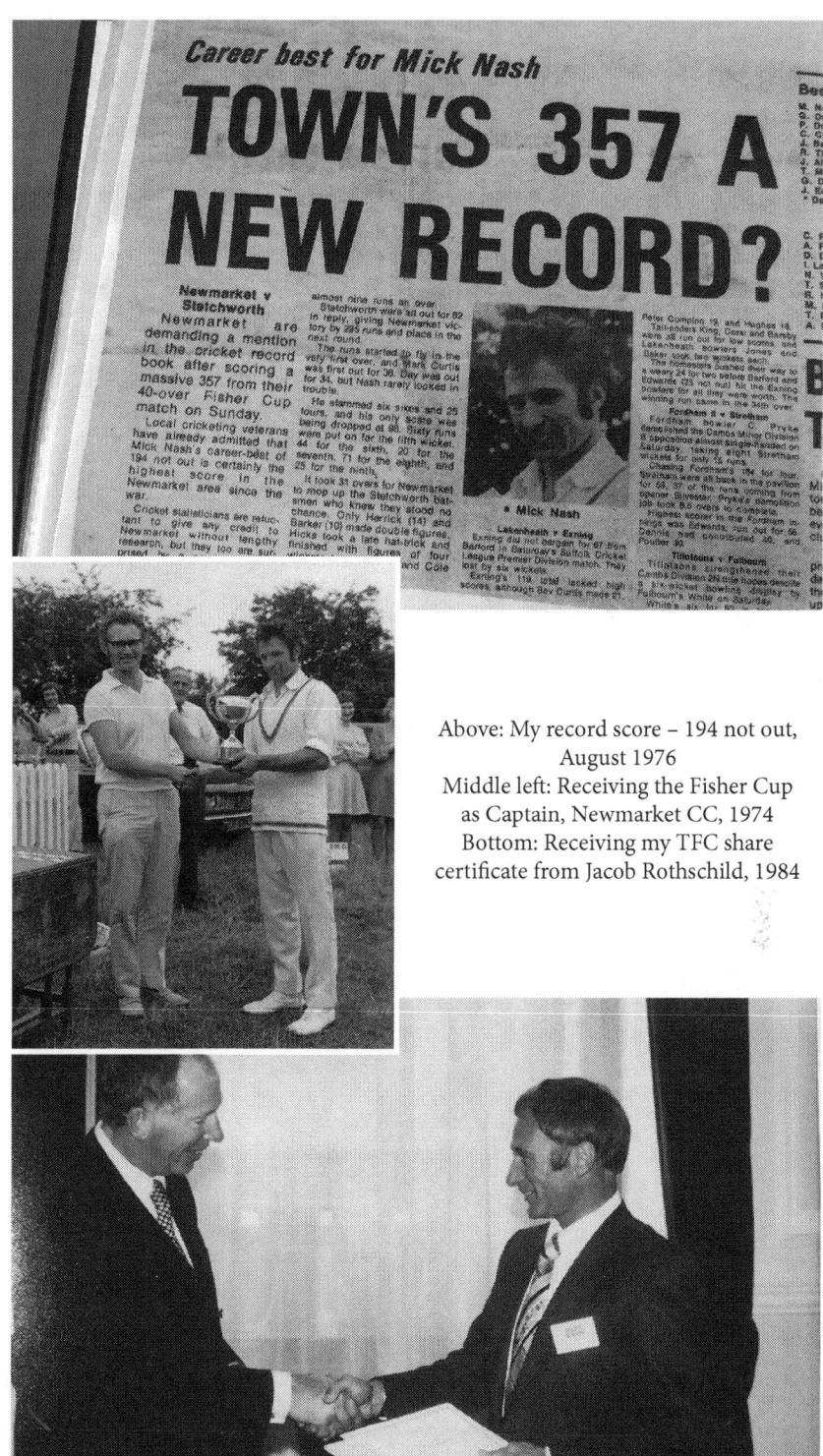

Career best for Mick Nash

TOWN'S 357 A NEW RECORD?

Newmarket v Stetchworth

Newmarket are demanding a mention in the cricket record book after scoring a massive 357 from their 40-over Fisher Cup match on Sunday.

Local cricketing veterans have already admitted that Mick Nash's career-best of 194 not out is certainly the highest score in the Newmarket area since the war.

Cricket statisticians are reluctant to give any credit to Newmarket without lengthy research, but they too are surprised...

• Mick Nash

Above: My record score – 194 not out, August 1976
Middle left: Receiving the Fisher Cup as Captain, Newmarket CC, 1974
Bottom: Receiving my TFC share certificate from Jacob Rothschild, 1984

Left: Boarding Concorde,
March 1986
Bottom left: As Managing
Director of Financial Planning,
Scotland March 1991
Bottom right: London
Marathon Finisher, April 1993

Above: Celebrating our 50th wedding anniversary on the Orient Express
Bottom: My 70th birthday party

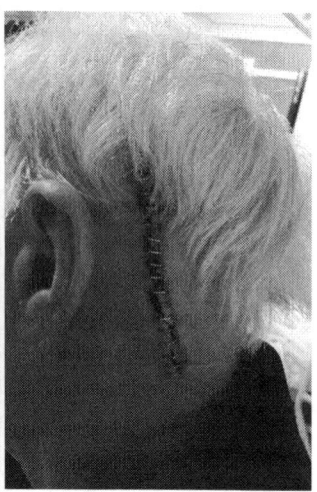

Above Left: My Last Munro
Beinn na Lap, July 2013
Above right: After the TN
operation, March 2015
Middle left: With my colleague
Alex Dowdalls & ICC
umpire Alem Dar
Bottom: Umpiring Pink
Ball T20 cricket

15

METAL DETECTING

I have always had a fascination with coins, particularly ones from the past, and have purchased several sets of pre-decimalised coins.

Whilst we were setting up The Bartering Company franchise, Andrew Hennell had mentioned he had arrived in Scotland a day before a proposed meeting to go metal detecting. Renting a cottage near Callander with his colleague, Jeremy Whittaker, they had been metal detecting near Stirling Old Bridge and Cambuskenneth Abbey. He showed me his detector, which had been made by a friend who was a specialist in electronics, and asked if I would like him to get me one. I had fancied having a go at this hobby but had never got around to it, so, I said, "Yes, please."

Two weeks later, Andew and Jeremy came to Scotland with my detector, which was made from various components, and showed me how to operate it. Along with his colleague, Jeremy, Andrew and I went out to Cambuskenneth Abbey one evening at dusk. He said that research showed it was a good site as Jeremy had previously found a Roman phallic symbol there. We all detected for an hour or so, mainly digging up ferrous metals, when Andrew spotted a vehicle parked in a gateway to a field. Not having gained permission to detect on the site, we decided to pack up and leave. As we drove away in Andrew's car, the vehicle parked in the gateway began to follow us. Speeding up, Andrew decided to outrun it and asked me for directions to try to lose it. I instructed him to head for the centre of Stirling where we could lose them on the back road to Stirling Castle. Thinking we had lost them, Andrew pulled into the car park of the Highland Hotel. However, two minutes later, the chasing vehicle pulled in beside us. Jumping out, the occupants asked us what we were doing in the field, so Andrew showed them the metal detectors in the boot of the car. Thinking they were undercover police, Andrew asked them who they were. At this, the two people started laughing and revealed that they were salmon protection officers. They had been observing us detecting through night-vision binoculars, and, from a distance, it looked as though we were trying to net salmon from the nearby River Forth. We all had a good laugh, shook hands, and went back to mine for a drink. That was my first experience of metal detecting.

Metal detecting was very much a learning process, understanding the different signals coming through the headphones. Without this knowledge, one spent a lot of time digging up ferrous metal (iron) as opposed to non-ferrous metals such as gold and silver. Very soon, my detecting became more productive, and I found hammered silver coins, pre-decimalised coins, and rings, instead of lumps of rusty iron. Unlike in England, the Romans spent less time in Scotland, so the finds were fewer. One always had to get permission to detect on land and keep away from historical sites. I joined a club called the Federation of Individual Detectorists as it provided me with a membership card and public liability insurance cover. This added to my credibility when seeking permission, which was usually granted.

One evening while detecting on a field opposite Lecropt Church, I unearthed a hammered silver coin, yet to be identified. When leaving the site, I swung the detector around the gateway and got a solid signal. Digging up the lump of earth, I found buried within a George III 'Cartwheel' penny – a huge coin for people to carry around in the 1700s.

My first Roman coin was found in England near a place called Wandlebury, one evening whilst detecting with Andrew and Jeremy. The coin was a bronze from the reign of Constantine I (306–337). Though not particularly valuable, the feeling of holding something a Roman would have lost over a thousand years ago was remarkable. That is the true fascination of metal detecting: when you get a strong signal then comes the anticipation of what may lie beneath the surface. Who would have lost it? Did they know they had lost it? Did they return to find it, without success?

The fascination of finding historical objects became an obsession, so, with the landowner's permission, I would go out at night when I was less likely to attract attention. When detecting during daylight hours, this always happened, people asking what you were doing and if you had found anything. I detected in people's gardens, parks and recreation grounds, but only ever found pre-decimalised coinage and gold rings.

Beaches were also good sites as people regularly lost coins and jewellery in the sand and water.

My first detector did not perform very well near salt water, so I purchased a waterproof one that would detect in the water. Whenever we went on holiday or I was at an overseas conference, the detector, in its travelling case, came with me. This led to some interesting finds after people saw me running the detector over the sand. One such occasion was in Antigua when a family came over and asked me if I could help them find a piece of jewellery. It was a family heirloom, and they had lost it while sunbathing. I asked them roughly where it was so that I had a starting point. They made lines in the sand in the search area, and I detected all day, but without success. It was not until a day later that I found it: a gold chain with a family crest. By this time, they had gone home but had given me their contact details. I returned home and left a message on their answer machine, saying I thought

I had found it and asked them to send me their address. Sadly, they never made contact, so I still have that piece in my finds collection.

On another occasion I was in Mauritius after an MDRT meeting, doing some detecting on the beach, when a young man came over, and said, "Does that thing find gold?" I informed him that it did. He then said he was here on his honeymoon and had lost his wedding ring in the water while swimming. I asked him to identify the area where he had lost it. He directed me to the shallows, about 50 yards from where they had been lying on the beach. I first checked all the sand and then the water. I searched for two days but with no luck. Then, on the third day, I found it – he had told me it was engraved with their names, so I knew it was his. By then, they too had returned home but had given me their Jersey address. Once home, I carefully packaged the ring, sent it by registered delivery, and enclosed a note with my phone number and address. I never heard back from them, which was disappointing after the effort I had made to find it, especially as it was his wedding ring.

Another eventful occasion occurred on the island of Bali. This was during another break after an MDRT meeting when I went along with my waterproof detector. Bali is an Indonesian island with some lovely beaches of black volcanic sand. I had tried detecting early one morning with no success, so returned in the early evening to try again. I was met with a beach littered with broken coral – the outgoing tide had pulled all the sand off the beach. I decided to continue detecting and soon discovered old Chinese coins by the handful. As I went further into the water, I started to find rings and similar objects. There were so many coins that I gave some away to a couple of friends in my group. The coins were different shapes and sizes with holes in them. When I returned home, I decided that on my next visit to London, I would take them to the British Museum for identification. A few weeks after handing them in, I received a written report to say that the coins were indeed very old. The museum had identified and listed the different dynasties the coins represented: Tang Dynasty (618–907), Song Dynasty (960–1127) and Ching Dynasty (1644–1911). Museum staff are not permitted to value any items, so to this day I do not really know whether they have any monetary value.

As for the rings I found, another specialist informed me that they were the result of Hindu burial customs where the deceased person would be placed on a funeral pyre for cremation. That person would wear their rings and would have a necklace of coins placed around their neck. This explained the holes in the many coins I had found. Knowing this, I really felt guilty for taking home the coins and rings.

I no longer take my metal detectors abroad; since 9/11, the security around hand luggage has intensified. And putting detectors in the hold as luggage is not good for the electronic components, due to the cold conditions when flying at 35,000 feet.

I still have my detectors, but they are rarely used, unless I get a call from someone who has lost some jewellery in their garden or whilst crossing a field during an event they have attended. I am always ready to help, and, if successful, gain a lot of satisfaction in seeing them reunited with their precious item and the memory it evokes, which is often far more important than its monetary value.

16

CLUB FOOTBALLER

Football was the winter game that took over when the cricket season ended, usually around the first week of September when we returned to school after the long, six-week summer holiday. Football, or soccer as it later became known in my schooldays, was played throughout winter, right up to the first week of May, the last match always the FA Cup final at Wembley. My interest in football began at an early age; it was the 1953 Cup final, later dubbed 'The Matthews Final', between Blackpool and Bolton that most inspired me to want to play competitively. It was no coincidence that my first pair of football boots, purchased from the Co-operative Society store in Newmarket with my mum's dividend vouchers, carried the Stanley Matthews autograph.

Cheveley had a team which played every Saturday in the Bury and District League. Together with my school friends, I supported them at home matches which were played on the recreation ground. Occasionally, we would go to away matches because my older cousins were sometimes selected to play. I remember the goalkeeper, a big man called Ron Weir, Jacko Searle, the centre forward, and the Manderton brothers. These men were like household names to us youngsters and whom we hoped to emulate one day.

From September to April, most weekdays after school were spent at the Cheveley recreation ground, picking teams and having what was termed 'a kickabout'. Every Wednesday afternoon, the senior class walked from the school carrying football boots to the recreation ground. Here, two of the eldest pupils were nominated captains, and, in turn, selected their team from the remaining pupils. I was an extremely competitive player, always trying to win the ball. One day, Mr Moore said:

"Michael, if you continue to tackle like that, one day you will break a leg."

He was referring to the way I led with my right leg, leaving it exposed with no body weight behind it. How prophetic that turned out to be!

He must have seen some talent in my football ability, as he nominated me to take part in a Cambridgeshire schoolboys' trial. The match was held at Bottisham one Wednesday afternoon, Mr Moore taking me in his own car. It was quite a daunting experience, and I didn't play very well so was not offered another opportunity.

It was not until I was 15 that I started to be selected for what was termed Cheveley's Sunday team. Friendlies were arranged with other teams from the Newmarket area. For some reason. the Saturday team had been disbanded, so no football league team now existed. My older schoolfriends had gone off to play for neighbouring villages due to the lack of support in Cheveley, whilst others had passed the eleven-plus and were now going to a grammar school in Soham, a village just outside Newmarket, where they played for the school. These Sunday fixtures continued for a couple of years, usually with teams from Stanley House, a Newmarket racing establishment. This meant we all had to get our bikes out to cycle down to Newmarket for the game. Richard Swann, a local lad who had been playing in the team for the village of Gazeley, decided he would try to reform the Saturday team. An inaugural meeting was held at the Cheveley Star and Garter pub (which has since burnt down). The meeting was a success, and Richard became the secretary. The newly formed Cheveley FC was admitted to the Suffolk Border League, as well as the Morris Harvey and Bert Brown Cup competitions.

All these matches were played on a Saturday afternoon. I became a regular member of the team and enjoyed the competitive matches, scoring many goals from my position on the left wing. I also got sent off – the only time in my footballing career – during a local derby league game against Woodditton and Saxon Street. I had kicked out at an opponent who had been kicking me, the other player's misconduct unseen by Mr Davey, the referee. Ironically, I was to play for Woodditton and Saxon Street a short time later.

Cheveley FC became established once again, and, in 1958/59, went through to the final of the Snailwell Cup. This competition was played on the grounds of Snailwell Park. An encouraging first half performance against Balsham FC saw us draw 1-1. The second half was different as they changed their goalkeeper for a player from the forward line (this was before the days of substitutes) and he ran in three goals, so we lost 4-1. A year later, the team became depleted as two of the team – Geoff Gammon and Alan Moore – went to university. My cousin, Neville Godfrey, who had to do national service, went into the RAF at the same time. With no new players replacing these three, Cheveley FC was once again disbanded.

Barry Howe, an agricultural engineer whom I knew from my time working for W.A. Challis, had heard of Cheveley FC's demise. One day, I met Barry while visiting his workshop to get a repair done on a sugar beet harvester. It was then that he suggested I might like to play for Woodditton and Saxon Street FC. This was the nearest village to where I lived, so both my brother and I joined the team. We did not know it at the time, but the next few years became the most successful for the club, progressing at it did up the Cambridgeshire league by winning the divisions each year and the Wilkin Shield competition. This was followed by the Cambridgeshire Lower Junior Cup. The club also twice won team of the month; an award sponsored by the Cambridge Evening News.

I was now playing left-half which I thoroughly enjoyed as it involved a defensive role as well as picking up the ball midfield to supply the forwards. I scored several goals from this position – mostly from outside the penalty area – by running on to a pass back and smashing it into the back of the net. My brother, Dennis, also proved to be a handy player in the forward line, scoring many goals.

This success continued until 1966 with the Woodditton and Saxon Street team appearing in many cup finals. We did not win all of them, but I have a collection of winners' cups and runners-up trophies to remind me of those successes. Fond memories indeed.

I was working at Sprite's Caravans when Paddy Kearns, a supervisor at the company and a committee member of Exning United FC, approached me one day at work. He said that the club would like to sign me as a player for the next season. This club competed in the Cambridgeshire premier league, which was three divisions higher than the league in which I currently played. There were also other players in that team working at Sprite's whom I knew. This influenced my decision. So, when the 1966 season kicked off, I played left-half for Exning United. The pace of the game was much quicker than I had been used to, with less time to distribute the ball; it was several games before I really got used to the higher standard. The club also played in the senior cup competitions, and the FA Amateur Cup, as it was known in those days.

After a full season, I was made captain the following year and moved to the position of left-back. The club had a new set of sky-blue kit, and John Parfitt, a player, had taken on the role of player manager.

John was a particularly good coach who modelled himself on Matt Busby, the Manchester United manager at the time, even wearing the same type of raincoat on the touchline. John had been in the departure lounge at Munich Airport on 6 February 1958 on his way home from doing national service in Cyprus, when he met the Manchester United team, known as the Busby Babes. They were in transit from Belgrade and were waiting to board their flight to Manchester. The team had successfully eliminated Red Star Belgrade FC in a European Cup match to reach the semi-final. Sadly, as we know from history, the Manchester United plane crashed on the third attempt to take off. There were 23 fatalities, including some of the most talented players ever to wear the famous red shirt. John, who saw them all in the departure lounge, was one of the last people to get all their autographs before he boarded his flight to London.

My time as captain at Exning United was full of highlights, and some disappointments. The club reached a few cup finals but never won any. It was during a floodlit cup match at West Row FC on 5 November 1968 when my footballing days came to a sudden end. I had gone in to tackle for the ball, leaving my right leg exposed. A West Row player, following through, caught me just above the ankle. There was a loud crack, the sound like breaking a dead stick, and instantly I knew what had happened, just as my former headmaster, Mr Moore, had predicted 10 years earlier. In 1961, I had broken a player's leg whilst playing for Cheveley FC at Chippenham Park against a team called The Borderers. The player was called John Claydon, and his leg had also cracked like a broken stick.

As I lay on the ground, I saw that my right leg above the ankle was now at an angle – 90 degrees to where it should be. The referee, upon realising what had happened, immediately stopped the game. Players from my team and opponents rushed to help. I just shouted, "Don't touch me!" I grabbed my foot and straightened it. At that instant, the pain from the break was transmitted right up to my thigh and was excruciating. I was carried from the pitch on an improvised stretcher, which turned out to be an old wooden door, into the changing room. So, the game could continue.

Someone from the home club had phoned for an ambulance but because it was Guy Fawkes night, the ambulances were all busy attending to firework-related incidents. I lay in the changing room in serious pain; the upper leg could not support the weight of the lower broken part. The ambulance crew finally arrived an hour later, though it felt much longer. The match had now ended; I never knew the result. Easing my broken leg into a polythene-type sleeve, the paramedics zipped it up and filled it with air. This had the effect of taking the weight off the now useless lower leg, relieving the pain. As the ambulance made its way to hospital, the air started to leak out of the plastic sleeve. The pain returned and was only relieved by the ambulance attendant blowing into it to keep it inflated.

Arriving at Newmarket General Hospital 40 minutes later, I found the team manager, John Parfitt, waiting with my wife who was six months pregnant with Graham. John had left the match, driven to our house to inform her of what had happened, and then brought her to the hospital, so both were there when I arrived. At home, my mum and dad and two-year-old daughter, Michaela, were waiting for my return to let off some fireworks. I had promised them before I left for the game that I would be straight back as soon as the match ended so we could have a party.

I remember nothing else of that evening other than Kate holding my hand as I was transferred to a trolley and wheeled into the operating theatre, still wearing my football boots and kit. I was asked to count to 10 as the anaesthetic was injected to knock me out.

The next morning, I awoke to find my right leg in plaster up to my thigh, but it felt wonderfully comfortable after the horrendous evening before. A nurse was enquiring as to whether I could move my toes sticking out of the plaster, then informed me that both the tibia and fibula had been broken. I spent three days in hospital before being discharged with crutches. Six weeks later, I returned for the leg to be X-rayed, and the plaster cast changed. It was late February 1969 when the cast was removed completely. During that time, Graham, our second child, had been born on 3rd February. I had driven Kate to the hospital the evening before when she went into labour using just the left leg on the car pedals to drive.

After six weeks of physiotherapy, twice a week, I could once again walk without crutches. I had to walk in front of the lead orthopaedic surgeon, Mr Jamieson, and for the first few steps without crutches I thought my leg would fail me and I would fall over. As I walked towards him it felt quite strange, having relied on crutches for three months, but I was safely back on two legs. Mr Jamieson reviewed how the break had healed and informed me that being near the ankle, it could be vulnerable to breaking again if it received another serious blow. It was recommended that I should consider never playing football again. Anticipating this decision, I had already started attending courses to qualify as a football referee whilst the leg was still in plaster. I never played football competitively again other than to take part in the annual referees five-a-side indoor county tournament. I did, however, put a pair of football boots on once more for a friendly match at the home of Bury FC (now the site of a supermarket) – Newmarket referees versus Bury referees.

The boots I wore that fateful night, the laces cut by the medics for easier removal from my muddy legs, gathered dust in the cellar at Gleniffer for many years until August 2020, when I decided it was time they went, and I took them to the recycling centre.

The sky-blue sock that was cut away from the broken leg was returned to the club with my shorts and shirt. The sock was sown up for further use by the lady who laundered all the kit every week. However, I was told that when the kit was laid out for future matches in the changing room, no one would select that sock!

17

FOOTBALL REFEREE

Breaking my leg at 26 and being advised not to play again was a devastating blow; I had played competitive football every season since 1957. To stay in the game, I decided that I would try to qualify as a football referee.

I contacted Adrian Kidd, the Newmarket area training officer, who said a new course was about to begin. The courses were held at his home on a weekly basis. I attended for eight weeks, along with Michael Kirkby and Billy Lucas, two workmates from Sprite Caravans who were also keen to become referees. At the end of the course, the Suffolk examiner, Mr Burchell, came from Bury St. Edmunds to The Mount pub in Newmarket where an exam on the laws was to be taken. Candidates were also required to take a colour-blind test. I passed in March 1969, becoming a Class Three qualified football referee. My two friends, however, did not pass and chose not to re-sit the exam – a great shame.

Being a Newmarket resident meant that I had to register as a referee with the Suffolk Football Association. The nearest league for me to officiate for was the Bury and District Football League, which consisted of six divisions. I contacted the appointments secretary – Captain A.W. Britt – who sent me a list of matches for the first six weeks of the season, beginning in September.

I duly ordered the referee's uniform of black shirt with white collar, button-on white cuffs, black shorts, black socks with white tops, and black boots. With some trepidation, I looked forward to my first match. Before this, I had an opportunity to referee a friendly warm-up at Soham Town Rangers' ground. My kit had not arrived, so I borrowed an outfit from Jim Mason, another workmate from Sprite's, who had been refereeing for just over two years. The match went well, and I was pleased to have had the opportunity to assess myself with a friendly before doing a league match.

The first Saturday in September 1969 arrived, and my first competitive appointment was at Icklingham, a village halfway between Newmarket and Bury St. Edmunds. The match was a Bury and District League Division Three game. The match fee was twelve shillings and sixpence, plus travelling expenses – one and a half pence per mile. The match went very well and without incident. From then on, every Saturday I refereed a match. I loved it, particularly the respect players had for me, and the fact that I was still involved in the game. A year later, the Bury Sunday league was formed, so I registered with that league too. This meant an early start on Sunday mornings as the matches kicked off at 10.30am.

I was promoted to Class Two in my third year, after being assessed by Suffolk County FA assessors. This meant that I now refereed higher divisions and minor county cup matches. The following year, after further on-field assessments by the county assessors, I was promoted to Class One – the top level. I was now qualified to referee the top divisions and cup ties in Suffolk. This promotion also enabled me to officiate as a linesman on the Essex and Suffolk border and eastern counties leagues. (The clubs in these leagues had semi-professional players in their teams.) Further positive reports from clubs on my performance as referee, and assessments by observers, enabled me to progress from a linesman to a referee in these leagues, as well as the Cambridgeshire Premier League and Eastern Professional Floodlit League – known as feeder leagues. All this could lead to my eventual appointment to what was then the English Football League. Appointments were also received from Lancaster Gate, the home of the Football Association in London, for early round qualifying matches in the FA Cup, as well as intercounty matches appointed by Suffolk FA.

During the season 1977/78, I started to have problems with my left knee; the diagnosis was a cartilage tear that would have to be fixed. I needed it done quickly so I could return to refereeing. (I had to complete the required number of matches to remain on what had become the Magnet and Planet feeder league.) My walking friend, David Levy, told me about an orthopaedic surgeon – Mr Dandy – a Canadian who lived in Great Wilbraham, a village located a few miles from Newmarket. He had pioneered keyhole knee surgery with a quick recovery. David had recently had an operation for a similar problem so gave me the contact details. I made an appointment with Dandy and was booked into the Evelyn Nursing Home in Cambridge for the surgery on 16 March 1978. I was discharged the next day and began the rehabilitation programme I had been given. It was a complete success – I was back refereeing after five weeks. I completed my requisite number of feeder league games and looked forward to the 1978/79 season.

Refereeing gave me an outlet in the winter and kept me fit. I had a lot of respect from both players and my refereeing colleagues for my style of refereeing and management of the players. At the end of each season, I had my share of officiating most of the local cup finals: West Row Cup (the competition in which I had broken my leg), Snailwell Cup, Exning Charity Cup, Fordham Memorial Cup, Bury League divisional finals, and Bury Sunday league finals, plus Suffolk county appointments.

My refereeing highlight, however, was being appointed linesman for the 1979 Suffolk Senior Cup final on 25 April at Portman Road, home of Ipswich Town FC. The manager of Ipswich at the time was Bobby

Robson who later managed England to a World Cup semi-final. He was present that evening and welcomed the teams and officials to the club. It had been raining all day; the ground was looking waterlogged as I walked out with the referee and the other linesman to inspect the conditions. We decided that it was unlikely the match would proceed as Ipswich had an important football league Division One match on the coming Saturday against Tottenham Hotspur. As we returned to the dressing room, Bobby Robson met us, and said:

"It is wet, isn't it? I know how important this occasion is for you and the players, so I will arrange for the ground staff to fork and sand the worst patches so you can go ahead and get the match played."

What an ambassador for the game! His success as manager for Ipswich Town, and, latterly, England, was unsurprising. He was later knighted by the Queen for his services to football.

As the 1979/80 season came, I continued to referee every weekend – either for the Essex and Suffolk Border League or the Magnet and Planet League, and occasionally the Cambridge Premier League. Midweek matches saw me as linesman or referee on the Eastern Professional Floodlit League, which meant travelling to Kings Lynn, Wisbech, Stevenage and Bedford. Refereeing intercounty youth matches between Norfolk, Suffolk, Cambridgeshire and Hertfordshire also gave me the opportunity to savour the football league grounds in those counties.

Another benefit that went with the level of Class One referee was to be a steward at Wembley for England's international matches and FA Cup finals. For each match, the counties in England were asked by the Football Association to nominate two people, so I volunteered several times (it was only a two-hour drive from home to Wembley stadium). The duty of the stewards was to check that the supporters were in the correct seats shown on their ticket, then, once the match started, we could watch the game for free. (This was in the days before stewards with yellow Day-Glo jackets were employed.) I was able to see several internationals and cup finals. On 10 May 1978, Wembley hosted the European Cup final between Club Brugge and defending champions Liverpool. Liverpool won 1–0 after a close match. In the same year, the FA Cup final between Arsenal and Ipswich took place on 6 May. Being an Ipswich Town supporter, I managed to buy a ticket and was successful in being selected as a steward. Graham, who was nine, came with me. Ipswich were very much the underdogs against Arsenal but won 1–0.

During this time, I also become Newmarket branch referee's secretary which led to my becoming secretary of Suffolk Referees Association. This entailed monthly meetings in the winter months at Stowmarket, as well as attending the other county associations' annual dinners as a guest speaker. In my role as the Suffolk county delegate, I also had to attend the national conference each year. My first national meeting was at Liverpool in the famous Adelphi hotel. The following year it was held in Norwich on 16 and 17 June. This was the Diamond Jubilee Conference, marking 60 years since the formation of the Referees Association. Kate accompanied me and enjoyed the excursions around Norwich, which were organised for the ladies. In the evening, we both enjoyed the dinner and dancing with the other delegates and guests.

I was enjoying the county secretarial role and the responsibility, when in 1980 my job with Barclay's Life meant a move to their Manchester office. When we decided to settle in Poynton, Cheshire, I registered with the Cheshire County Football Association and received a referee's appointment. Unfortunately, the date clashed with a friend's wedding back in Newmarket (Keith White, my cricket vice-captain). I never did referee a match for Cheshire as we were only in Poynton until July 1981. I did not know it at the time, but my last match was 9 February 1980, when, on a return visit to Newmarket, I refereed an early round Snailwell Cup match between Moulton FC and St. Edmunds FC.

When we moved to Scotland in 1981, I supported Michaela who by then had become involved with athletics and needed transporting to cross-country races at the weekends. I never returned to refereeing, not even bothering to register with the Scottish FA. By then I was 38; one can only wonder how far I could have gone.

50 years later, I look at the conduct of players today and the way referees are jostled and questioned whenever a decision does not suit them. It is a shame that what was termed 'the beautiful game' is no longer the case; money has dictated the need to win. The laws are clear: the referee's decision is final; there is no point arguing or expecting the referee to change his or her mind. Respect for the official has gone and the penalties applied need to be enforced, with no appeals. As I write this, VAR (Video Assist Referee) has been introduced at the top of the game, whereby a panel of experts review every contentious decision, allowing the referee's original decision to be overturned.

I enjoyed my time as one of Suffolk's top officials for club and county matches but would not enjoy the game today where no respect is given, and authority is continually questioned.

18

CLUB CRICKETER

I have tried to pinpoint when my interest in cricket began and think it was when we lived in Great Barton. I would have been seven or eight when Dad cut out a pitch in one of the stud paddocks so I could have a go at batting and bowling with my brother, Dennis, and the children from across the road – Raymond and Janie Alcock. During the summer, every spare moment after school, the wickets, which were homemade, so too the bat Dad had fashioned from some fence railings, came out.

My interest progressed when Bert Hawker moved into the house opposite ours to work on Barton Stud. He was very keen on cricket and played for Great Barton village. Each home match he used to take me on his bicycle to watch; his wife, Nora, was the scorer. This increased my interest even further, as I thought this was great – all the players wearing white flannels and white jumpers. There were other boys at the match my age and we used to practice our own game outside the boundary whilst the big match was going on. Later, I learnt to score the match, which was also exciting, as it meant I got to have some tea with the players between innings.

A year or so later, Robin Hopwood, who was the stud groom's son at Great Barton Stud, heard of my interest and asked me to play in a match that he had organised with his friends from school (he attended a private school) against the local boys of Great Barton. The match took place on one of the stud paddocks where a pitch was prepared. The stumps and bails consisted of hazelnut sticks cut from the hedgerow. I batted number 11, using borrowed pads and a proper bat. I scored two runs by turning the ball down the legside. I was also asked to bowl a couple of overs, though do not remember taking any wickets. This match was played again the following year and took place on Great Barton recreation ground where I managed to hold on to my very first catch in a competitive match. A few days later, outside the house where I was practising my bowling, Robin Hopwood's grandad saw me, and said:

"With a left-arm action like that, keep it up and you will play for England."

He may have just said it to keep encouraging me, but I have never forgotten the comment.

I was later to play in a Great Barton Senior School match that year (the youngest junior to be asked to play), but I spent the whole match fielding; I did not bat nor bowl.

We moved to Cheveley in September 1952, so I started at Cheveley CofE school immediately. As it was the football season, I had to wait until the following summer before I got the chance to play cricket again. Fortunately, Mr Moore was very keen on cricket as well as football, so the school had its own cricket kit. Each Wednesday afternoon, all the senior class walked to Cheveley's recreation ground to pitch the stumps and pick two teams to play against each other. In addition to the Wednesday afternoons, Mr Moore allowed us to borrow the school kit when I organised matches against the local village of Kirtling. David Bailey, my good friend and talented cricketer, would organise and captain this team. The players would all cycle to Cheveley for an evening's match and then cycle back to Kirtling.

It was two years later that Cheveley started its own cricket team, one that had been dormant for several years. (Bill Hitch, who went on to play for Surrey and England, began his playing career for Cheveley in the 1930s.) The team started by playing friendlies against neighbouring villages, but it was not until I was 13 that I got selected to play. The match was against Newmarket 2nds, and it rained on and off for most of the day. This was in the days of plimsolls, so my feet got soaked during the first innings when Newmarket was batting, and I was crossing over in between overs to different fielding positions. I batted at number 11 and was caught in the slips, having scored just two runs.

I was then picked several times for evening matches which were 20 overs (today, many people think T20 is something new, but we played it in the 1950s). As they were evening games starting at 6pm, one could just get 20 overs a-side done by 9pm before it got too dark. My first real success came in one of those games against Hammonds, a work's side from Newmarket. I was asked to bowl halfway through their innings and took four wickets which included a clean-bowled, and a diving caught-and-bowled. I was proud of my caught-and-bowled; so much so that the next day I went back and rehearsed it when no one was around.

At the age of fifteen I became a regular in the Cheveley team, picking up my first trophy in 1958 when Cheveley won the Suttle Cup by beating Power Controls, a team from Newmarket. In that same team were two of my cousins, Reg Godfrey and Derek Hicks. I did not feature in the batting or bowling as Ron Martin, a slow left-arm bowler who was also a milkman who delivered in Cheveley, took most of the wickets in a low-scoring game.

Buoyed on by this success, Cheveley entered the Teversham Cup – for teams around Cambridgeshire – and two years later won that as well. I had by this time met Kate and was delighted when she came along to support us with her friend Pauline.

Cheveley as a club then started to decline as Alan Moore and Geoff Gammon went away to University and Neville Godfrey went into the RAF. I went to Cambridge Technical College and on Saturdays had a job as a baker's delivery boy, so I could only play in Sunday games. However, due to the religious Sunday observance, it meant matches had to finish at 6pm so very few were organised.

Cricket, however, was still my first sport in the summer, so I joined Kirtling CC in the neighbouring village. They only played friendlies on a Sunday which suited me, and in only my second year, I won the Best Bowler Cup for taking the most wickets. I had played for them for about three years when one day Stan Tredgett, a successful cricketer, called at my parents' house to ask me to play for Kennett and Kentford. This team was in the Higham and District league which was much more competitive than just friendlies. The matches were played on Saturdays, and I was now working for W.A. Challis where I finished work at midday. One year later, we were successful in winning the league, my bowling featuring in the success.

Kennett and Kentford then decided to seek more competitive opposition, so joined the Cambridgeshire leagues. This meant starting in Division 5b, which all clubs joining the Cambridgeshire leagues had to do. The club quickly progressed, each year winning each division, eventually being promoted to Division Two. This division was a tough league, with teams from around the Cambridge area. It also meant qualification for the Junior Cup, a very prestigious trophy named after Prince Ranjitsinhji, an Indian prince who had studied at Cambridge University during the 1890s. He went on to play cricket for Cambridge University, Sussex, and Test cricket for England. The final of this trophy was played on the number one pitch on Parker's Piece in the centre of Cambridge and was known as Hobbs's Wicket, named after Jack Hobbs, who became one of England's most successful opening batsmen.

32 teams contested the cup from the start of the season which had to be played in addition to league matches. In 1967, K&K (as the club had become known) were through to the final against Horseheath, a village a few miles south-east of Cambridge. Playing on the famous Hobbs's Wicket for the final had everyone excited, and, batting first, K&K posted a modest score. The opposition progressed towards the target through one batsman and the score got closer, until one of their batsmen, a left-hander who had been in a while and was looking comfortable, pulled a ball high in the air to me at deep fine leg. Judging the height and distance, I got underneath it and managed to hang on to the catch at the second attempt. All the team ran to congratulate me, and Percy Bird, the captain of the team, said:

"Boy, you've just won this match for us!"

How right he was, as the opposition came up a few runs short. Percy collected the trophy, and I opened a bottle of champagne I had smuggled into my cricket bag. One aspect of winning that trophy was that the names of all the team were engraved on the silver rings, which are presented with the trophy, for posterity.

We were successful again the following year, winning the final easily against Hardwick, a village six miles west of Cambridge. Batting first, K&K scored 136 runs and bowled out Hardwick for just 39 runs. This time my brother, Dennis, was also in the team. Looking to make it a hattrick of finals in 1969, we were easily beaten in the first round by Shelford. One local trophy that eluded me personally was the Gibson Cup, an 18-over prestigious midweek competition, with the final being played at Exning CC. We did get to the final one year but were beaten by Mildenhall CC. This was a great disappointment to us as Jimmy Watson, our long-time secretary, was dying of cancer and had been allowed out of hospital to watch the final. We would have loved to have taken the trophy as a final tribute to him.

The club managed to stay in Division 2b but started to lose some key players to Exning CC who had joined the Suffolk leagues, a higher standard. This was only natural as they wanted to play more senior cricket. I had married Kate by now and began playing midweek games for Newmarket, where we lived. They kept trying to persuade me to play for them at weekends as they had some particularly good friendly fixtures, but I preferred competitive cricket, stating that when they decided to play league cricket, I would play for them. This happened in 1973. Newmarket had joined the Suffolk league structure, playing in Division One. I played in the first competitive league match in which Newmarket had ever played: away to Brockley, a village in west Suffolk. The match was won easily; my left-arm swing bowling being the deciding factor, taking nine wickets for just 12 runs.

The following year, I was elected captain of Newmarket, and we gave good account of ourselves each season, eventually winning the Suffolk League Division One in 1977. However, there was no promotion to the Suffolk Premier League – it remained a closed shop by the clubs already in it. Prior to that, in 1973 we won the Fisher Cup by beating Cherry Hinton in a low-scoring game; a match that looked lost, when, batting first, we were all bowled out for 62 runs. I, however, knew we had the ability to win the match if we took early wickets, a belief that had come from my competitive nature. We had them struggling at 38–5 when a recovery got them to 56–6. They now needed only seven runs, with four wickets in hand. Due to some excellent fielding and bowling, they came up four runs short, all out for 58. I had taken 6–25 in 13.2 overs. I was immensely proud to collect from Dr Fisher, the donor's son, the first trophy Newmarket had ever won.

Midweek cricket saw us collect more accolades, winning the Bottisham midweek and Fordham midweek leagues, plus the Fairhaven and Ingham cups and six-a-side tournament.

Newmarket Cricket Club achieved success it had never enjoyed before; we embarked on two overseas tours to Guernsey, as well as tours to Oxford. The Guernsey tours were extra special as the club president, Lady Butt, formerly of Newmarket, now lived in Guernsey. In between matches, she invited the whole team, plus members of Guernsey Cricket Association, to her garden parties. Not only did the players travel to Guernsey, but so too all their families, including children. To finance this, the club held jumble sales, bring-and-buy stalls, newspaper recycling, and special draws. The club was in good shape, with a wonderful ladies' committee, as well as the general committee.

The success became infectious; so much so that it was decided to replace the existing pavilion, first built in the late 1800s. This would be achieved by members doing the work involved – purchasing a prefabricated building to replace the old one. So it was, on an Autumn morning in 1976, work began. The new pavilion, complete with showers, was officially opened by Lady Butt on 8 September 1977.

My best success as a cricketer came during my captaincy of Newmarket. It was in 1976 when I did what is known as the double: scoring 1,000 runs and taking 100 wickets. The double still stands. I also hold the highest individual score of 194 not out (the previous holder was Bill Hitch). I had also taken 100 wickets in three successive seasons and three hat-tricks. One such hat-trick was unique – it was the last two wickets of a match against Witchford and the first wicket of my next match, when I clean bowled David Bailey of Kirtling, my great friend and keen rival.

My job with Barclays Life gave me flexibility to play more cricket, so, I went on two tours to Holland with Tillotson's Cricket Club as a guest player in July 1976 and 1977. I was also playing for Barclays Bank Cambridge District midweek. This was a successful side captained by my hillwalking friend, David Levy. On one of those tours (22–27 May 1977), we were based in Guildford. We played several bank districts, winning each one. The cricket was of a remarkably high standard as we came up against several minor counties' players; my left-arm swing bowling being particularly useful in getting out several opposition batsmen.

However, in 1978, Newmarket did not follow up the success of 1977, finishing third in the league. 1979 was to be my last season as a player and captain for Newmarket due to a career move, buying our home in Poynton in 1980.

On 29 February 1980, Newmarket Cricket Club held their annual dinner, whereupon Kate and I were presented with a cutglass whisky decanter and glasses in appreciation of my contribution as captain, and Kate's as a valuable member of the ladies' committee.

Poynton CC had two elevens – a first and second – and played in what was the Sondico Cheshire League. They also had something I had not before encountered: an overseas professional, Duleep Mendis, who later went on to become the first captain of Sri Lanka, previously Ceylon. Their ground was opposite to where we lived, so I went along one evening to practice and played in an early midweek match, taking three wickets in as many overs. I was then selected for their second eleven match the following Saturday. Roy Harrison captained the team; a real disciplinarian who insisted on players' boots being whitened before every match. I was asked to open the bowling and remember taking a couple of early wickets. I played most of the season in the second eleven but had one match in the first eleven, which was a much higher standard than I had been used to at Newmarket.

In one second eleven match away to Unsworth, a team in north Manchester, I had not opened the bowling but was kept back. With the opposition on 37–6, I was asked to bowl and had remarkable figures after just five deliveries: the first ball just outside off stump, the second clean bowled the batsman, the third was caught behind, the fourth was clean bowled (hattrick), and the fifth also caught behind. I had taken four wickets in four balls and Unsworth were all out. Having achieved previously more than one hattrick, this was the first time I had taken four in four balls – a feat not achieved before by a Poynton player.

Playing for Poynton was an interesting two years, playing on some good grounds and good pitches. I only played half the 1981 season as I was travelling back and forth to Scotland, arriving too late to play on the Saturday. It was disappointing as Mike Greatorix had become captain of the second eleven, a much more accomplished cricketer than the previous captain.

We moved to Scotland on 20 July 1981. I was then aged 38 and drove down to Williamfield, Stirling county's ground, with Graham to watch a match before the season ended, but I did not pursue this any further. My Saturdays were now taken up with supporting not only Michaela but also Graham, who had taken up cross-country running.

It was three years later, April 1985, before I played again, and this came about purely by chance. It was the start of the season when Linda Moodie, my newly appointed secretary at Target Life, commented that I used to play a bit of cricket. When I confirmed that I had, she said that St. Modans CC, a local Bannockburn side, were looking for players. I decided to go for practice one evening, after which I found myself in the team playing the coming Saturday.

St. Modans played in what was known as the East of Scotland League and were in Division Five. They had high ambitions of progressing through the leagues to the first division. My left-arm swing bowling became successful, and I was soon topping the club averages each season. One highlight was winning the Small Clubs Cup. This was a remarkably close match between our opponents, Strathmore CC, they needing only eight runs off the last over. I persuaded the captain, George Pollock, to let me bowl as I had previous experience of how to keep the batsmen from scoring by bowling a tight line. The opposition ended up four runs short; St. Modans had their first trophy.

Future years saw them make progress, finally ending up in East League Division One in 1991. This division consisted of the top Edinburgh teams such as Grange, Carlton, Royal High, Heriots, and many more, each of these clubs employing overseas professionals. It was in fact the top league in the East, so St. Modans had finally made it, playing against the top sides in Scotland.

I was now 48 and still physically fit, but, after 35 years of bowling, the sport had started to take its toll on my left shoulder, as well as damage gained to both my knees. I was, however, selected to play in the first match against Grange and succeeded in trapping their opening batsmen LBW. It was my only wicket of the match. This standard of cricket was much higher than I could cope with after so much wear on my left shoulder, so, after three matches I dropped down to St. Modans's second team. This suited me for a few seasons as my son Paul had started to play regularly, proving to be a very capable slow bowler who could spin the ball both ways.

I went on to become captain of the third team for two seasons before going back to captain the second team. The young players I had brought on as juniors were not getting selected every week due to ageing players still wanting to play. I discussed the situation with them, the result being that they wanted to change clubs and move to neighbouring Clackmannan County Cricket Club which played at a very picturesque ground in Alloa.

The 1996 season started. I was selected for the Clackmannan first eleven as the club had just withdrawn from the counties league due to the reorganisation of Scottish cricket, losing a lot of players. After two years of a mixture of first XI and second XI, I was elected captain of the second XI. Paul was now playing regularly, and I could make sure he got a fair amount of bowling experience and coaching, along with others of his age. There were also several other senior players in their twilight years making up the team, so it was a good balance of youth and age. In 2000, we won the ESCA League Division Five after some thrilling games, with Paul playing a significant part as vice-captain. I had struggled with a left shoulder problem throughout the season, resorting to painkillers during the games, so, knowing I was about to retire, I arranged an end-of-season barbecue for the whole team at home to celebrate the success.

A private consultation in October 2000 with Gordon MacKay, a knee and shoulder specialist, revealed a split rotator cuff which was unlikely to get better (in his words) without an operation. I decided to have the operation but had to postpone it until two days before Christmas, as I was about to embark on a trip to Sri Lanka to see England play a Test series.

The day after my return from Sri Lanka, Graham drove me to Ross Hall private hospital in Glasgow where the operation was performed, and, two days later, I was discharged, my left arm in a sling, in which it had to remain for the next six weeks.

It was early in 2001 when I received a phone call from the Clackmannan Cricket Club president asking if I would stand for election as captain of the first team for the forthcoming season. I thanked him for the offer but said I had decided to retire and umpire full-time instead. I also said that I was disappointed that no one had been in contact to ask how my operation had gone (not a single member of the club had telephoned!).

Two years later, I still missed playing. This was when I heard about the XL club. This was a team of cricketers over the age of 40 who played regular friendlies against private school teams and other organisations to further the game of cricket. I decided to join but played only four games before my left knee gave way at The Tryst, Stenhousemuir CC, after I opened the batting and scored 38. It was back to see the surgeon Mr MacKay, who performed keyhole surgery to remove torn cartilage tissue. After playing cricket for six decades, I finally called it a day. I no longer have my kit after donating it to a young asylum refugee, who is showing much promise as an under-15 Scotland player.

In September 2017, I suggested a Newmarket CC get-together to mark 40 years since winning the Suffolk League Division One. Keith

'Chalky' White, who had been my vice-captain, and I corresponded by email and listed the names of that team and other club members. On Sunday, 24 September, 40 years to the day, 17 members, players, and wives from 1977 assembled at the Heath Court Hotel in Newmarket for a private lunch. It was a great success, enjoyed by all those present; memories were exchanged and past highlights remembered. I thanked everyone for attending and asked that we remembered those players who were no longer with us, including some ladies who had played such a great part in that successful club during the 1970s.

The event concluded with a poem written by 'Chalky' White on 24 September 2017:

1967 was when it all began.
When I arrived at the practice nets
And was introduced to Stan.

Uncle Mac always drove the tractor
And thought he was the ticket,
Until one day while batting
He said, "Shucks, I have forgot my box"
When the ball hit his middle wicket.

The teas prepared by the ladies
Were always second to none.
Egg and onion sandwiches,
Sausage rolls, Victoria sponges
were very soon all gone!

David Game, Barry Linford, Bill Lemar –
Just a few names from early years.
Even if the cricket was bad,
They would always down a few beers!

650 not out, pints that is,
Were consumed on the 1970 Cumbria tour,
So, it came as no surprise
When some of us fell asleep
Behind the dressing room door.

We were entertained on the Guernsey tour
By president, Vilma, Lady Butt.
Her butler served us with exotic drinks,
So, it was therefore no surprise
That we all ended up half-cut.

Some great friendly matches
At Fenners, Pembroke and St. John's
Did not totally satisfy our needs.
So, when Mick Nash came along,
We joined the Suffolk leagues.

Many competitive matches were to follow,
And some defeats were very hard to swallow.
But under Mick's driving force
The victories began to flow.

Even against Bub Grant,
We really gave it a go!

Finally, we won the league
And proved we were the best.
It will not go down in Wisden
But at least we won the Test!

And now just to complete this verse:
How the years have seemed to fly.
I for one hope one day
We all team up again,
On that great cricket ground in the sky!

19

UMPIRE

I was enjoying being captain of Clackmannan 2nd XI, especially given that my youngest son, Paul, had become a particularly good right-arm, off-break bowler with the ability to flight a very disguised leg break. When I was not getting teams out, Paul was. As one local newspaper headline once stated, after we had both contributed to a match-winning performance: "Like father, like son."

My left shoulder had increasingly given me problems while playing and I knew that I'd have to retire. So, I started umpire evening classes in the winter of 1998. I had considered coaching, but, having been a football referee, I felt I had the right temperament to umpire and give something back to the game. During matches, I had often grabbed the white coat when I was not batting (when it was down to the side batting to umpire their own team when neutral umpires had not been appointed). I enjoyed the classes and passed Level 1, a written paper. I was pleasantly surprised how much of the 42 laws I did not know and signed up the following winter for Level 2. In between learning, and while still playing, I umpired some East League matches and realised how much I enjoyed being involved.

The Level 2 course was much more detailed than the first and a pass mark of 85% was required. I narrowly missed this in 1999, and, as the laws were being revised, there was no further opportunity to sit the exam again until 2001. This time I easily achieved the pass mark.

By now, I had done more umpiring in between playing; my left shoulder giving me serious problems. I saw Gordon McKay, the orthopaedic surgeon, the same surgeon who had performed the surgery to my left knee. An MRI scan revealed a split rotator cuff. (This sits on the top of the shoulder socket like an upside-down golf tee.) To avoid surgery, cortisone injections were tried, but to no avail, so the only solution was surgery. I was booked into Ross Hall, a private hospital in Paisley, Glasgow, on 22 December 2001.

As the season drew near, I notified the umpires' appointment's secretary, Sandy Scotland, that I was to stand full-time, and I received appointments in the East League. The following year, I was appointed to the National League and remember clearly my first match: SMRH versus Hillhead, a Division Two match. This was my first complete season as an umpire – something I wish I had done earlier – though playing outweighs standing as an umpire for upwards of seven hours.

As I progressed, I was appointed to more important matches and finally made the grade to Premier League. The first match was Uddingston versus Clydesdale. My colleague that day was Mac Wyle who had had the distinction of umpiring the National Village final at Lords many years earlier. He told me after the game that I had performed well and would be given more Premier matches.

A few years earlier, Cricket Scotland had amalgamated all the various leagues to form what was known as the National League, with a Premier Division and Divisions One and Two. The best teams made up the Premier League, the teams featuring the players who represented Scotland in international matches. The pressure of umpiring Premier matches was very intense, as each team usually had an overseas professional and an unpaid overseas amateur. Not only was knowledge of all the 42 laws of cricket essential, but managing the players was equally as important. My former experience as a soccer referee now came into its own. Also, having played the game for 50 years, I understood the mentality of what players were experiencing in volatile matches.

Standing with experienced colleagues such as Les Redford, Sandy Scotland, Mac Wyle and John MacGregor was an honour, as they had umpired matches in which I had previously played. Living in Dunblane meant I could travel to matches east or west, and as far north as Aberdeen, as far south as Dumfries. I was rewarded with umpiring the Small Clubs Cup final in 2005, exactly 20 years after I had played in that final as a player for St. Modans Cricket Club. This time, as umpire, the match was one-sided and John Templeton, my umpire colleague, and I had an easy match.

I had stood with John on several occasions, particularly at Arbroath and Broughty Ferry, Forfarshire's ground, where it was always a late return home as John liked a beer. (I usually ended up driving us back in his car.) John was a compulsive smoker and sadly died in 2014. He had been a Stirling County player and member and reminded me on more than one occasion that instead of playing for St. Modans CC when I came to Scotland, I should have played for his team.

Apart from the National League matches, which took place on Saturdays, there was the Scottish Cup. This tournament commenced towards the end of May, starting with the top 64 teams on a knockout basis. My first match in this competition was Heriot's FP versus Fauldhouse. My colleague was Graham Sutherland, known as 'Tubby', due to his portly size. He commenced play with his famous phrase: "Gentlemen, let's play." Sadly, Tubby died in 2016, but I will always remember his wonderful sense of humour and politeness with the players.

It was a Scottish first-round cup match in 2000 – Edinburgh Accies versus Uddingston – when my colleague, Gordon Whitelaw, and I realised after the first innings had been completed that the pitch was shorter than the statutory 22 yards. We completed the second innings and then measured the pitch: it was short by two yards. A junior match had been played previously, and the same markings had been used as a template. The match was replayed the following week with different umpires, but the result was the same: a win for Uddingston.

Umpiring midweek evening matches from mid-May until July also became a regular feature; firstly, with the Masterton Trophy, an East of Scotland competition, and, latterly, the West League Cup and Rowan Cup run by the Western District Cricket Union (WDCU). John MacGregor, who appointed the umpires for the WDCU, realised I could easily get to the matches from Dunblane in the evenings; over the years, I umpired all the finals of these competitions more than once.

The National UK Village competition takes place on Sundays during the season, the final played at Lords, the home of cricket, in September. This competition for village clubs was won by Isleham in 1978, a team based just outside Newmarket. Freuchie CC were the first team from Scotland to win the same trophy in 1987. I was very honoured to be asked to umpire the Northern Zone final, when Freuchie again reached the last eight in 2006. They were playing Sessay CC, a team from Yorkshire, the same team Isleham had beaten in the 1978 final. My colleague was Les Redford who, by then, had been umpiring for over 20 years. The match was played at Freuchie on a glorious afternoon, watched by a crowd of more than 500. Freuchie was easily beaten, but it was a wonderful experience for me to umpire and experience how much this competition meant to the locals, even in Scotland where cricket is not their number one sport.

I became a regular member of the Premier panel of umpires and looked forward to each Saturday, standing with different colleagues at all the Premier grounds. Arbroath CC became my favourite where I was always assured of a good welcome, and the teas were second to none. Gordon Whitelaw from Larbert and I were often paired together to save clubs' travel expenses, especially when going to Aberdeen. On one occasion, we arrived at the ground (now designated as the most northerly ICC ground) to find Sky Sports there doing a programme on local clubs. They filmed the whole match against Grange, for which we were promised a recording. We never received it.

I was once again one of the umpires, when, in July 2013, Sky Sports were recording a series called Local Rivalries, shown before the start of Test match coverage. This would feature my match – Clydesdale versus Ferguslie – the two cricket teams with as much rivalry as football teams Rangers and Celtic. My colleague on this occasion was Eric Young who had been umpiring for about the same amount of time as me. The match was a Pro 40 Cup match played at Clydesdale CC in front of supporters from both sides. The match was competitive, with Clydesdale batting first. They posted a total of 175 in their 40 overs for Ferguslie to chase. The match came down to the last over, Ferguslie requiring six runs off the last two balls. It was the penultimate ball that was hit towards the long on boundary for six, when the Clydesdale fielder managed to knock it back into play whilst the batsmen had run two. My colleague, Eric, signalled six, only to then call dead ball and consult me for a correct decision. I stated that the fielder had stopped the ball going over the boundary and he should revoke his last signal and indicate two runs had been scored. This he duly did, and Clydesdale were the winners. This was all captured by the Sky Sports cameras. When the programme was shown, David Lloyd and Ian Botham, the voiceover presenters, stated that the umpires had made the right call. Even more important was the fact we were both being assessed by Paddy O'Hara, a boundary assessor from Ireland who was establishing whether Eric was suitable for the ICC second tier panel.

Up to season 2016, I had regularly umpired Premier League matches as a Premier panel umpire every Saturday. Then Sandy Scotland, who managed the appointments for the Scottish Cricket Officials Association (SCOA) and had done so for many years, was replaced by the Domestic Officials Committee (DOC). This committee consisted of members from the East umpires and West umpires. I was a member of both but was elected to the committee by the West. The appointments would now be made separately by each area – the WDCU (Western District Cricket Union) would appoint umpires for the West, and the ESCA (East Scotland Cricket Association) would appoint the umpires for the East. Living in Dunblane, I was equidistant to both so would umpire two weeks for the East and two weeks, West. Though I continued to be appointed for Premier matches in the West, I only umpired one Premier match in the East. This was very disappointing as I wished to maintain contact with the clubs from both sides of the country.

I was now one of the longest-serving umpires, only four other umpires (both East and West) having served longer. I had never umpired the Scottish Cup Final, but I was always hopeful; some colleagues who had not been umpiring for as long as me had been appointed to this final. I had umpired the Challenge Cup Final twice and the Plate Final, so was hopeful of being nominated for the 2016 final. I later learned from the West umpires' chairman that I had been nominated, along with a good umpire friend, Clive Allen, from the East. However, we were both turned down by the chairman of the DOC as we were considered too old! The same teams compete for the final of the Scottish Cup, for which we both umpire regularly, so this decision did not make sense. I thought this was unfair, considering the service I had given, and made the decision to stop umpiring altogether before then changing my mind: I would umpire for one more season – 2017. During the closed season, the chairman of the DOC had categorically stated at a meeting in early April that age would be no barrier to domestic appointments, provided the person was able and capable. So, I was once again hopeful of being considered for the Scottish Cup Final.

The season started on the last weekend in April, with me umpiring an East championship match at Carlton. This was followed by several Premier matches in the West and a first-round Cup match on 14 May at SMRH. This was all over in less than two hours, SMRH batting first all out for 22 runs.

It was not until July that I was appointed to any East Premier matches, and then three in successive weeks: Carlton, Watsonians, and Falkland. During each match I was to be observed by my colleague – twice by Gary Nicol, and once by Clive Allen. My instinct told me their presence was to establish my performance in readiness for the Cup final. My feeling was further enhanced when Les Redford was tasked to do a boundary observation in the Falkland game.

The first match, Carlton versus Glenrothes, was reduced to 38 overs a side due to overnight rain which had leaked under the covers. It was an exciting finish, with the scores tied. I thought I had given some good decisions, and the match had gone well. Gary, my colleague, thought so too and gave me a good report. The second match between Watsonians and Aberdeenshire was a harder game to umpire, with lots of appeals and unnecessary backchat. But again, I thought I had done well, getting my decisions correct and stamping on any unnecessary chat which has unfortunately become part of the game. Gary again wrote a positive report. The third match was at Scroggie Park between Falkland and Carlton. I arrived early at 10.45pm to find the boundary assessor, Les Redford, already present. The covers were on the pitch as it had started to drizzle. My colleague, Clive Allen, arrived at 11.00am by which time the drizzle has ceased. We did a boundary inspection and arranged for the boundary at the far end of the ground to be re-marked to avoid a wet area. Arranging for the covers to be pushed back, a small wet patch was evident where a short ball might pitch, so we asked for it to be dried. As the pitch had not had a chance to be cut, we allowed it to be cut and rolled and informed both captains that the start time would be delayed until 12.30pm. Once the groundsman had finished his work and marked the crease lines, the covers were put back as the weather didn't look promising. Clive and I got changed and came out at 12.25pm to find the Carlton players, who were batting, ready to go. However, there was no sign of the Falkland team. We knocked on their changing room to discover that they were still wearing their warm-up kit. The captain's explanation was that as the covers were still on, he did not think the game would start at 12.30pm. Clive told him in strong words that the start time remained the same and that they had better hurry up and get changed. The match started at 12.40pm, the opening Carlton batsmen keen to play. Drizzle threatened but it remained dry as Clive called, "Play."

Both opening bowlers had no problem with their run-ups or landing area but were displeased that the ball was damp and needed drying after being hit into the outfield. It then started to stop-start drizzle several times, but the conditions were neither dangerous nor inclement, so we allowed play to continue. The Falkland bowlers then took three quick wickets, one an LBW decision from me. Carlton was 43–3, and, suddenly, the Falkland bowlers were no longer complaining about a wet ball and were happy to continue. The drizzle increased, so Clive and I had another discussion and decided to give it another over, this despite the Carlton captain, who was also the Scotland captain, voicing his opinion to Clive from the boundary. On the last ball of the over, from my end the Carlton batsmen played the ball into the covers, set off for a single, and slipped. After I had called "Over", we again discussed the situation and called for the covers. No further play was possible; the drizzle became heavier for the rest of the afternoon. Les Redford, who, as previously mentioned was doing a boundary assessment of both Clive and I, came into the changing room as we were getting changed. He said he thought we had got the decision to play on right; he said too many of the newer umpires readily call games off when they should at least try to get a game on.

Two days later, Clive and I were both asked to submit a report as to why we allowed the match to continue following reports from the captains, who each gave us a rating of poor. I did not send in a report but asked to see the captains' reports and that of the assessor. Eventually we were provided copies which did not reflect the true situation – the Falkland captain's report had been completed by someone from the club who was not even at the game! We were eventually informed that both captains' reports would be ignored. The assessment from Les Redford, which we had not been given until I asked for it, gave us both a good assessment, considering the difficulties over the weather.

I met with Clive after the season had ended as I had again been nominated by the West of Scotland Association of Cricket Officials (WOSACO) as the nomination from the West for the Scottish Cup Final. This was overturned by the chairman of the DOC after a member from the East had objected to me being given the final on what he called 'sentimental' reasons, citing that as the East had selected their nomination, the West should provide someone on the Inter Regional Umpires Panel (IRUP). The chairman of WOSACO put forward my case, but to no avail. I was then nominated by WOSACO for the playoff final between the Eastern Premier champions and the Western Premier champions – Watsonians versus Prestwick. I had umpired both clubs several times over the years, and, more recently, during the 2017 season. Again, my nomination was objected despite me having more experience umpiring both clubs than the umpires who both eventually got the final. The chairman of WOSACO argued my case again but was overruled by the chairman of the DOC. He was pressurised once again by the East appointments' officer who was insisting that both umpires should be Category One. (I could easily have been Category One for the season but choose to drop down to Category Two to allow younger umpires to step up.) This was another disappointment for me and really closed the door for ever on being able to umpire either the Scottish Cup Final or the playoff final. There are umpires who have done these finals more than once, which I think is unfair. It should be an honour and reward for service, provided the person is capable, and one should only be permitted to umpire the final once. It was November 2018 when I decided to resign as WOSACO's development officer from the DOC. It was not about me; it is not how democracy works in committees. When one person objects and is then supported by the chairperson to override the majority, who knows how many times that is going to happen?

I umpired during the 2019 season, after being appointed to East and West Premier and some Division One matches. The season 2020 was affected by the COVID-19 pandemic with all matches being cancelled.

It was November 2020 when I received a phone call one evening from Bob McFarlane, chairman of the DOC, notifying me that a proposal was being put forward to form one body for cricket officials in Scotland. I was asked if I would take on the role of Development Manager for what would be known as CSMOA – Cricket Scotland Match Officials' Association. I would be responsible for choosing a development officer for each region – East, West, and North – from the available umpires who would report to me and a mentoring officer.

I thought carefully about the offer, which would be voluntary, and decided to accept. I appointed my development officers for each area and a mentoring officer, but this only lasted for a year. I was then asked to be the appointments' officer for the Western District Union matches (excluding the Premier League) for season 2022. I was tutored on a software programme called WTU (Who's the Umpire), enabling the appointments to be made, and successfully appointed umpires for that season.

In March 2023, I met at a café in Bridge of Allan with the developments officer, who had taken over my earlier role, and the WTU appointments' officer to discuss the forthcoming 2023 season. I was asked if, during the forthcoming season, I would be available 24/7 to be able to reappoint umpires in the event of late call-offs. (The previous season, due to late call-offs, matches had proceeded with only one umpire or none!) I stated quite clearly that I would not, as I was retired and did not always have my electronic devices to hand to check cancellations at short notice. The meeting concluded and I returned home. The season commenced with appointments being made for the WDCU; no one had had the courtesy to inform me that I was not required.

I umpired during the 2023 season after my hip had healed following an operation, enjoying the friendships built up over the years with the players and club officials. Towards the end of the season, I was appointed to a match at Irvine Cricket Club. My colleague was Gavin Gemmell, a long-standing umpire of many years. Gavin was 86 and I was 80, so, together, we had a combined age of 166, a record for Scottish cricket, possibly the UK.

The season of 2024 commenced during the last week of April, but I had just had cataract surgery to my right eye. Unfortunately, due to a genetic condition called Fuchs' Endothelial Corneal Dystrophy, the removal of the cataract made my sight worse. Despite applying eye drops for several months, my vision didn't improve. Therefore, despite remaining a full member of CSMOA, I did not umpire any matches.

In November 2024, I paid privately for an operation at the Moorfield eye clinic in London to have a cornea donor tissue transplant. As I write this at the beginning of April 2025, the procedure has been a complete success. I am therefore intending to umpire a limited number of matches during the upcoming 2025 season.

20

DARTS PLAYER

As a young boy, darts were something I had occasionally thrown at a cork board we had at home when living at Sandwich Stud. I became more competitive, when, as a teenager, an occasional evening was spent at the Red Lion pub in Cheveley. I was naturally left-handed and enjoyed the competitiveness with my other teenage friends. Games were the best of three legs; you had to start with a double from 301, then another double to finish. Being able to subtract each score quickly from the total left was important, so as not to upset your throwing rhythm. It was many years later that Kate told me my mental arithmetic skills in being able to subtract scores quickly and accurately, had impressed her when we were going out together!

The Red Lion pub had a darts team that competed in the local Licensed Victual Association (LVA) League and played other pub teams every Wednesday during the winter months. Teams consisted of nine players who were drawn to compete individually. The evening was a good social occasion; one week the match played at home and the next, away. The Red Lion's landlady, May Mayhall, would provide cheese and onion sandwiches for the players as a refreshment during the evening. The winning team would receive two points, so, at the end of the season, the team with the most points would be declared the league champions.

Though not a member of the team, I would usually be present when the darts matches were taking place. Licensing laws prevented anyone under the age of 18 from being allowed in the public bar where the competition took place (I was only 15). However, the lounge area of the pub did allow underage members to meet socially, so I was usually present on the competition evenings. I was in the lounge one evening when the team were playing The Turf, a local pub from Newmarket. The captain of The Red Lion's team, George Thomas, said to me:

"You are going to have to play as we are a player short."

One team member had not shown up and the match was tied four– all. I was now going to be the ninth player. Grabbing my darts, which were behind the bar, I went into the public bar to find the opponent I was playing: The Turf's star player, Fred Lee. Stepping up to the mat and making sure my right foot was behind the eight-foot line mark, I threw a dart at the bullseye. The closest to it went first; my opponent was nearer. Unlike world darts competitions shown on TV where the players do not have to throw a double to start, the LVA rules required players to start with any double to chase down 301. My opponent was away first time with double 20. As a left-hander, I preferred to throw across the board to my favourite double number, 13. My first dart was in double 13, followed by triple 20, and single 20 –106 scored, leaving 195. I cannot remember how the first leg went from there, only that I needed double 10 to finish, which I got, before my opponent got down to his double. The second leg is also a distant memory except the finish: I needed 60 and aimed for single 20, then double 20, and won. I received much backslapping and cheers from the spectators, though not from the opponents who had lost the match. I was 15 and should not have been allowed in the public bar, but, as a darts player, it was just regarded as a social occasion if I did not drink alcohol.

I was then selected for the team every week – home or away, if I was available. It was The Red Lion's most successful season – they went on to win the LVA Championship at the finals' night at The Carlton ballroom in Newmarket (now sadly demolished), defeating the other group winners 5-0. I was not even required to play, it being such a comprehensive win!

Two years later, The Red Lion entered the darts national team event sponsored by The People, a national Sunday newspaper. This was a team event of eight, each throwing one after the other, alternating with your opponents over five legs of 1001. I was one of the team members, and, after defeating teams in the early rounds, we got through to the area finals. This was held at Chatteris's working men's club in 1960/61 and we were victorious.

Every winter, I played darts for The Red Lion on a Wednesday, becoming captain when I was 18, and, on a Friday, played for The Plough, a pub in the neighbouring village of Ashley who competed in a different league.

In 1965/66, I paired up with my cousin, John Godfrey, to enter the pairs' championship. We became champions for The Red Lion, enabling us to qualify for the LVA pairs' competition which was played throughout the season. We won through all the early rounds, and, at the Turner Hall in Newmarket on finals' night, we beat our opponents by two straight legs to lift the trophy.

Any practice was usually on a Sunday morning, soon after the pub opened at noon, until around 2pm when it was time to leave for Sunday lunch. Pairing up with another player, you would play a leg of 501 against another pair. If you won, you then stayed on the board to take on the next pair who had chalked (scored) your game. As long as you kept winning, you kept playing, which could be for the whole time, until the pub closed at 2.30pm. Should you score 180, the maximum, the pub awarded a cigar. I accumulated quite a few but did not smoke, so would give them to friends whenever they came to visit. Sometimes there was a lengthy list of people waiting to play, so pairs matches were abandoned in favour of 'Shanghai', 'killer', or 'halve-it', the rules of which can be found online. These games involved everyone, and there was usually a bonus for the winner. It cost a shilling to take part, and the winner took the kitty.

Once I was married to Kate and moved to Newmarket in 1964, the journey to Cheveley each Sunday became a bit of a chore. I stopped playing for The Red Lion competitively, instead playing for the team at Sprite Caravans where I then worked. They had also entered a darts team in what was known as the Stradishall and District League. I was selected from over 800 workers to play for the firm's incredibly competitive team. I held my own in the team; I was a regular player when we finished runners-up in 1969. A year later, in 1970, we were the champions. I left Sprite's employment in 1974 so have only occasionally thrown a dart in a friendly match since. My set of darts is old-fashioned compared with today's models and are still in the wooden case made at Sprite's. They remain in the glove compartment of my car just in case! I still retain my winners' cups and medals as a reminder that darts was an important part of my social life at that time.

As I finish writing this chapter, 16-year-old Luke Littler has just reached the final of the World Darts Championship, with a prize of £500,000. Darts is now a major TV viewing sport, and there are darts academies where players can go to practice seven days a week; not like in my day, when you either practised at home or waited until the pubs opened!

21

MICHAELA JANE

On 2 June 1966, our lives as a married couple would change forever when our first child, Michaela Jane, was born. Michaela had been conceived nine months earlier whilst on a touring holiday in Cornwall.

We had been living at 12 Heathbell Road, Newmarket, for nearly two years, when, on 1 June, I had taken Kate into the maternity ward at the then Newmarket General Hospital. I was not allowed to stay and returned home to finish decorating the kitchen (we had decided to wallpaper one wall). Our neighbours on each side – the Edgeleys and the Hockleys – were keen to know what was happening, but it was not until the following day that I could let them know that we had a healthy baby girl, who weighed just over 6lbs.

It was not until the evening visiting hours that I could see her, and, even then, had to wait until the dads were called by the staff nurse to see their offspring. All the newborn babies were in the nursery at the end of the ward. It was an amazing moment seeing this tiny baby with a label on her ankle denoting her surname. I was allowed about 10 minutes in the nursery before being ushered back to my wife's bedside. What a proud and wonderful moment – to think that we were now responsible for another human being.

Kate had to stay in hospital for 10 days, the requirement in those days for a firstborn, so each evening I would visit and go through the routine of waiting until the staff nurse allowed us down into the nursery. Eventually the 10 days passed, and I put a carrycot into the car as I prepared to collect both mother and baby. Arriving back home, both sets of grandparents were soon visiting, though they had also visited in hospital. I was given just a day's maternity leave from Sprite's, soon having to return to work, leaving Kate to manage the baby. A significant memory was the first time Michaela could sit up without cushions all around her; the next when she took her first steps.

Our daughter was enrolled into a nursery class at the Turner Hall in Newmarket at the age of four. Kate spent a lot of time teaching her to read using the 'Peter and Jane' books; so much so that by the time she started school, Michaela was quite advanced. Before that, she would be taken to Sunday school at Cheveley Church by the children from next door to my mum and dad at Broad Green.

We took a couple of holidays in her first two years: once at Cromer in a residential caravan which we shared with our honeymoon friends from Jersey, Vic and Sandra, and the other with my mum and dad at Clacton-on-Sea

Michaela started school at All Saints Primary in Newmarket at the age of five and was soon bringing home stars for her work. It was there she found a passion for sports. As the annual sports day arrived, I built a rudimentary high jump so she could practice in the garden with her friends. She also showed an aptitude for colouring and drawing.

During the summer, when the weather was good, bits of wooden panels and cardboard boxes would be assembled on the back lawn, used to build a tent for Michaela and other children of the same age who lived in Heathbell Road.

In 1976, we moved to 25 Elizabeth Avenue on the other side of Newmarket. This meant a change of school for her – St. Felix Middle School. Once again excelling at sports, she still holds the long jump record which will never be beaten, as, sadly, the school burnt down many years ago after we moved to Scotland. Whilst there, in her last year, Michaela was part of the chorus for the school musical 'Joseph and the Amazing Technicolor Dreamcoat'.

When my job took me to Manchester in 1980, we moved to Poynton in Cheshire. Now aged 13, Michaela had to attend Poynton High School. She made friends easily and one friend, Joanna, introduced her to track athletics. Once a week, I would drive them to either Stretford or Altrincham athletic tracks for training. This lasted until 1981, when, once again, my job took me further north to Scotland. Michaela was upset as she had to leave friends behind, and, more importantly, the athletics coach who had trained her.

We settled into a home in Dunblane; Dunblane High School became home to Michaela's final school years. Her running took on a new dimension when she joined Glasgow Athletics Club and we found that the coach, Ronnie Kane, was excellent. Sadly, Ronnie died suddenly two years later.

Following her final year at Dunblane High School, Michaela went on to study physiotherapy at Queen Margaret College, Edinburgh. Her first job was at Chase Farm Hospital, London.

She married George McCallum in August 1992 whom she met at Central Region Athletics Club. From that marriage we have two wonderful grandchildren: Stuart Jamie, born 15 September 1995, and Rory Andrew, born 14 February 1998.

Michaela and George now live in Casares, Spain, where they run yoga retreats.

22

GRAHAM PETER

We were blessed with a second child in the early hours of 3 February 1969, when Graham Peter was born. Taking Kate to the Newmarket Maternity Hospital the evening before has special memories. I still had my right leg in plaster following the break in November 1968. Kate had felt the contractions, which had started late in the evening, so I asked our next-door neighbours to come over to look after Michaela. I worked out how to drive our Hillman Minx with my right leg in plaster; as the left leg was the one controlling the clutch, it was a question of knocking it out of gear then using the left leg to brake. We made it to the hospital without incident, and, with crutches, I helped Kate to the ward where I rang the night bell. A nurse came and led Kate away, asking me to wait outside in a cold corridor. I waited for what seemed ages then decided to go back home. It was a sleepless night until Kate called me at around 8am to say that we had a son.

This time, it was only two days before we were all together again as a family at home – 12 Heathbell Road. Michaela adored her baby brother and was always eager to help with his bathing and getting things for Kate when she was breastfeeding him. Michaela had also been breastfed which was believed to be the best for newborns, helping them to get some immunity for later in life. Graham progressed well, until one evening when he was nearly three. He developed a fever and was very lethargic; Kate was nursing him when she suddenly felt Graham go very stiff in her arms. I grabbed him from her, rushed to the back door, and set him down on his feet on the cold paving slabs. Immediately he responded and became more alert. Meanwhile, Kate had rung for the doctor who arrived within minutes. I can still recall the vision of Dr Walker from the Newmarket practice leaping out of his Land Rover, jumping over the flower borders and sprinting into the house. He examined him and immediately stated that we were to take him to hospital. Arriving at the hospital, Graham was taken from us to be examined and diagnosed with double pneumonia. He was detained overnight while the nurses monitored his condition. We were allowed to see him before having to leave. This was a stressful moment, but, as we looked at him, he said:

"There is a ghost in here."

He was now much more alert, and, with the nursing staff wearing white masks, thought they were ghosts. The next morning, we learned that he had had a high temperature throughout the night, but a nurse kept vigil whilst sponging him down. He remained in hospital for a week in his own room within the geriatric ward. Kate and I took turns being with him every day, keeping him occupied. His favourite task was completing a jigsaw puzzle of a train with no more than a dozen pieces. This he did over and over, interspersed with short breaks to walk down the ward to see the older patients. Eventually, after a week, he was discharged. Ever since that episode, we were always concerned whenever he had a bit of a temperature.

Like Michaela, Graham started school at All Saints Primary. He hated it. It was always a struggle to get his coat on when the time came to leave: "I don't want to go to school. I don't have to!" Eventually, he got used to the idea, and, like Michaela, did very well there.

From All Saints, the next school he attended was St. Felix Middle School. This was only for a short period before we moved to Poynton, and then on to The Arns at Dunblane. Graham did very well with his education at the Dunblane schools and had his sights set on being a veterinary surgeon. However, he went on to do accountancy, gaining his degree from Heriot Watt University in Edinburgh.

Graham's main hobby was fishing, and he would go to the River Allan near Kinbuck, a short walk from The Arns. He became very adept at salmon and trout fishing; so much so that he would tie his own fishing flies then sell them to his schoolfriends.

In 1986, together with me and John Doherty, a work colleague, we walked the West Highland Way, finishing on top of Ben Nevis, raising money for Cancer Research. Five years later, Graham and I walked the Southern Upland Way, another long-distance walk, of 212 miles.

It was in his teens that Graham got the passion for hillwalking. This was during a weekend when the Trimarc group visited, inspiring him to complete all the Munros, which he did in 2002 (number 3982). He then started fell running and eventually ultra running, taking part in events across Italy, Switzerland, France, Madeira and Spain.

It was whilst at school in Dunblane that another pupil, Nicola Ingles, caught his eye and they started going out together. They were married on 5 June 1996 at St. Marys Church, Dunblane, and they too have given us two wonderful grandchildren: Andrew William Michael, born 19 October 2003, and Rachael Lucy Anne, born 2 January 2006.

23

PAUL MICHAEL

Eight years after Graham's birth, Kate discovered she was pregnant again. We both had no hesitation in looking forward to either a baby sister or brother for Michaela and Graham. Paul Michael was born 6 September 1977. Paul's birth coincided with Newmarket CC winning the Suffolk League Division One title, the first time in its history. As captain of the club, this was a double celebration. Michaela and Graham were delighted with their baby brother, and, when not at school, helped with all the care that a new baby needs.

Paul was christened on Sunday 7 May at All Saints Church, Newmarket, where we were married; Tony Day, a family friend, acted as godparent.

A particular incident occurred which is still vivid in my memory and one I relate to Paul. It was 5 December 1977, and Paul was asleep in his pram in the back garden of 25 Elizabeth Avenue, when a US Airforce F111 jet crashed just 100 yards away. We were used to aircraft flying over Newmarket due to the proximity of the two US Airforce bases at Lakenheath and Mildenhall. On this day, however, I heard the scream of engines above and then a thump as the aircraft smashed into the ground. I said to Kate, "A plane has crashed near here." I went outside and saw billowing smoke at the back of houses on the next street. Reaching the scene, I climbed the fence where the aircraft had crashed in a vacant stud paddock and was blazing away. The aircraft had suffered hydraulic failure, so the pilot and navigator had ejected, leaving the aircraft to plummet to the ground, narrowly missing a school. A US Airforce helicopter hovered overhead, telling people to keep away in case of further explosions. Part of one wing had ended up hanging from the corner of a nearby house. Thankfully, no one on the ground was killed; the pilot and navigator survived.

Paul started school at Dunblane Primary in 1982, ending his education at the senior school. Unfortunately, he did not get his grades at Dunblane High School to go on to university.

While at school, he had done morning newspaper deliveries for the local newsagent, and then, at the weekends, worked for the local pizza takeaway. It was the owner of the pizza takeaway who persuaded him to work for him full-time after he left school. A year later, Paul realised this type of work was not for him. He thought about his future and decided to leave. He continued his further education at Perth College, and, with some private tuition, gained enough qualifications to attend Napier University in Edinburgh. He successfully graduated with a degree in mechanical engineering.

After working for Welsh company, Hyder Water, Paul gained enough experience to start his own company in 2008: Caledonia Water & Environment. He later changed the name to Caley Water Ltd. With premises in Edinburgh, the company now employs several staff.

Paul was a particularly good cricketer; a slow right-arm bowler able to turn the ball both ways. We used to practice in the garden together at The Arns, having had an artificial turf strip laid between practice nets. He was a member at St. Modans as a junior, together with other schoolfriends from Dunblane, before becoming a regular player for St. Modans 2nd XI. He had changed clubs to Clackmannan County, not getting enough of an opportunity to bowl when he was selected for St. Modans 1st XI. He was a member of the successful Clackmannan County 2nd XI, winning the Division Seven title in 2002. The success was due in no small part to Paul's bowling ability to take wickets at crucial times.

Paul's main sporting activity now is long-distance running, training hard for ultra running events.

He met Sally Liddell from Alloa in 1998. It was 10 years before they were married at Dundas Castle, Edinburgh on 5 May 2008. Their daughter, Clara Annabelle, was born 4 November 2015, becoming our fifth grandchild.

24

BEEKEEPING

The benefits of honey are well documented; not the supermarket honey, but natural honey extracted by a beekeeper from a colony of bees.

Whenever I saw the sign 'local honey for sale', I would stop and purchase some. Spread on warm toast for breakfast, the taste is unrivalled, determined by the flowers or plants the bees have been foraging in. It can also complement many dishes during the cooking process.

It was December 1981, our first year in Dunblane living at The Arns, when we decided to spend the Christmas break in our old hometown of Newmarket. Returning after the break, we pulled into the gate at The Arns and noticed that the burglar alarm light on the panel beside the house was flashing. Unlocking the front door, we were met with the sight of dripping water everywhere. It had been a particularly cold week in Scotland with snow and ice in abundance. This had caused the cold-water pipes and supply tank in the roof of the cottage to freeze. When a slight thaw came, the pipes burst, flooding the upper ceiling which had collapsed with the weight of water. The property was unhabitable.

I had previously stayed at the local hotel, Dunblane Hydro, whilst commuting before we moved from Poynton, so, as a family we stayed there for several days whilst a local building firm conducted repairs. It was a local man, Allenby Bain, who was painting one of the repaired ceilings, who told me our site was a great place to keep bees. I said to him that I had always fancied keeping bees, and he said, "You get a colony, and I'll start you off." I thought nothing more of it, until, several weeks later, I was at a Barclays Life meeting in Manchester and one of the bank liaison representatives, John Roberston, who lived in north Manchester, mentioned that he had a colony for sale. Agreeing a price, I arranged to visit late one evening to collect them.

This was in early May 1983. I arrived home from his house at dusk, by which time most of the bees would have returned to the hive. Fixing all the hive parts together with brackets, and blocking the hive entrance, they were loaded into my company car – a Morris Ital estate. John was a very experienced beekeeper, so, taking his advice, the bees were given a container with a feed of sugar syrup which would last them on the journey back to Dunblane. Pulling on my veil just in case any bees did escape on the drive north, I set off, arriving back in Dunblane just after midnight.

The next morning, I called Allenby, whom I had told the previous day that I was collecting a colony. He came to The Arns, and, together, we lifted them out of the car, siting them on the other side of the burn, which ran through the property, away from the house. Over the next few weeks, he taught me how to inspect the hive, manage the frames of bees, and look for any sign of diseases, such as deformed wing virus, foulbrood, chalkbrood, and nosema, the most common at the time. Another important job was to control the bees' instinct to swarm as this would mean a reduction in the honey crop.

By the end of August, the box containing the frames of honey, known as a 'super' Allenby said, was ready for extracting. Not having an extractor himself, Allenby borrowed one from the Dunblane & Stirling Beekeepers Association of which I had become a member. Using a knife dipped in hot water, each frame was de-capped (slicing of the wax), exposing the liquid honey which the bees had sealed. The frames were then inserted into the extractor – a stainless-steel drum – two at a time. The handle of the extractor was then turned so that the centrifugal force spun out the honey. Once all the frames were extracted, the honey was allowed to settle before being strained through a muslin cloth and bottled into jars. For the very first time, we now had our own honey. The first season produced 48 jars which I was told was an excellent return. Having taken the honey from the bees, which was their winter food supply, it meant that for them to survive until next spring, an alternative had to be provided. This was in the form of syrup, which was granulated sugar mixed with boiling water, allowed to cool, and then put into a feeder placed inside the hive.

In the winter months, Kate and I attended the Association's meetings to learn more from other beekeepers, who all had their own ideas on the best way to keep bees and improve the honey returns. Allenby gave me a useful piece of advice: "Listen to what everyone has to say and then make up your own mind as to what suits you best."

For the first few years, my bees were very productive, until a disease called Varroa spread from the Asian honeybee (Apis Cerana) into the European honeybee (Apis Mellifera). Finally, in 1992, it arrived in England. Two years later, due to the importing of bees, it had appeared in colonies in Scotland, and, a year later, in Dunblane. Initially, there was no known treatment for what became known as Varroosis, so any colonies infected had to be destroyed. The varroa mite, no bigger than a pinhead, attacks and feeds on honeybees by attaching itself to the body of the bee, then weakening the bee by sucking the fat body. As the mite can only reproduce in honeybees, the only solution was for the colony to be destroyed. Fortunately, I never had to have a colony destroyed, as, by the time it was evident in my bees, a form of control had been discovered. This measure involved placing Apistan chemical strips in between the brood frames once any honey had been removed. Later, a more effective treatment using oxalic acid as a fumigate became more effective. However, as this was dangerous to humans, it had to be conducted with a fellow beekeeper, both wearing a special chemical mask.

I did acquire further colonies from beekeepers who had decided to give up keeping them – from Callander, Alloa and Milngavie – but never had more than three colonies in total. Two years before moving from The Arns, I went to check the hive one morning only to discover that all the bees had gone; no swarming had taken place, they had just disappeared. This had been happening to other beekeepers; similar stories were also being reported from the USA where the explanation was the use of nicotinoids. This was a chemical that was being used to coat the seed of oil seed rape, prior to it being sown in the ground. Although it was effective in improving the oil seed rape crop by eliminating bugs which savaged the flowers of the plant, it was being passed onto the bees when foraging the bright yellow flowers for nectar. Eventually, the use of nicotinoids was banned.

I did not get another colony until two years after we moved to Gleniffer. In the meantime, I had attended a beekeepers' course at the Dunblane Cathedral Halls as I thought a refresher course with beginners would be useful. This proved to be extremely helpful, as techniques, equipment and research had moved on since I got my first colony 25 years earlier. I paid a fellow member £50 for a small nucleus with a newly mated queen, collected it, and transferred it into a hive in the spring of 2008. I had asked the neighbouring farmer if I could site the hive in the corner of his field right next to our garden. This he agreed to but told me to make sure the hive was secure when cattle were in that field as they may knock the hive over. The colony progressed well, and I split the hive (when it was large enough) by removing the queen into a new hive with nurse bees, enabling the original hive to produce a new queen. The volume of honey never returned to the levels of my first hive, but at least I was helping nature with the pollinating of crops and flowers.

Whilst away on our annual Guernsey holiday in September 2018, the farmer had transferred cattle into the field and the animals knocked over the hive, the last remaining one (I had lost a hive the previous winter). The following spring, I placed an empty hive on the same site hoping to attract a stray swarm. Keeping a check whenever I was at the vegetable boxes, nothing happened until the end of June 2019; I was thinning carrots when I became aware of the sound of bees. Looking up, I saw that a swarm had come in the day before and were busy getting themselves established. Leaving them for a couple of days to settle in, I then inspected and found that it was a big swarm with a marked queen, so someone had lost a colony from nearby. Managing them with frequent inspections, by late August enough honey had been capped to extract. The result: 12 jars. Ensuring they were well fed with syrup for the winter, treated for varroa, mouse guards fixed, and the roof weighted down with bricks against winter storms, I looked forward to more honey the following year.

A friend helped me to inspect them in late February 2020 as I had broken my wrist falling from a ladder while cleaning the house gutters in late December. I needed help in removing the heavy bricks on the hive roof. Opening the hive, we discovered the bees were doing fine: the queen was alive; eggs and brood visible. Despite a good start to the weather for the whole of May, June became variable and wet with the result that only eight jars of honey were extracted in August. Once again, for the coming winter I ensured the hive was watertight, and the bees well fed, hopeful for a good honey crop in 2021. However, it was not until 2022 that I once again had a reasonable return of honey.

The changing climate is undoubtedly affecting honeybees; wet winters are worse than snow and freezing conditions, when the bees remain in a cluster, while the wet causes dampness, leading to several diseases. Season 2024 has been an excellent year for honey but now we have another problem on the horizon: the Asian hornet which has been making progress across Europe and has now been seen in England. This predator eats honeybees, so can destroy a complete colony. Visiting my daughter, who lives in Casares, Spain, last September, I met the local beekeeper who originally had 90 colonies. At the end of the summer, he had only 10 – Asian hornets had destroyed the rest.

Beekeepers in Scotland remain hopeful that the Scottish winters, though no longer harsh, may keep the Asian hornet down South.

25

CONCORDE

In the late 1960s came a joint venture between Britain and France: an agreement to build a supersonic passenger airliner that could travel at twice the speed of sound. Previously, this had only been possible with military aircraft. After many trials, at a cost of £1.3 billion, the first Concorde went into service in 1976, flying from London Heathrow to New York in just over three hours. Though the aircraft only had seating capacity for 92–128 passengers, it had a cruising speed of 1,354mph – 23 miles a minute – faster than a bullet, and, at Mach 2.04, over twice the speed of sound; it had a take-off speed of 220 knots (250mph). Concorde became the pride of the British Airways (BA) fleet.

Of the 20 built, six were prototypes, the remaining 14 taken up between BA and Air France (AF). Despite other airlines originally placing orders, only BA and AF used them until 2003. The Americans and Russians had both failed in their attempt to build a supersonic airliner, but the joint venture between Britain and France was a huge success. Everyone wanted to experience this new wonder of travel whereby you could arrive in New York before you had left London, due to the different time zones. However, the cost to fly on this 'wonder of the skies' was beyond the means of most people, it being the reserve of the very wealthy. On occasion, BA would use it on the Edinburgh Heathrow shuttle route as a special treat. The airline never advertised when this would happen, though, so the chances of having a flight on it were very slim.

In March 1986, England were playing a five Test match series in the West Indies. It had always been my ambition to see a Test match in every test-playing country ever since I was a small boy, when I would listen to commentaries on the radio from these faraway places. Finally, at 43, I was on the point of fulfilling my dream. I had decided to fly to Barbados at the end of March to see the 3rd Test. Kuoni, the travel company, had put together a package for the five-day trip which I saw advertised. I contacted the agent and booked the trip. There was, however, an option to take the return flight on Concorde for an extra £100 (providing there were vacant seats). At that time, Concorde would make a weekly trip to Barbados, flying the wealthy people who had properties there for weekend breaks, and would not always return with a full payload. I took the option of returning on Concorde and looked forward to my holiday in Barbados.

England lost the Test match in only three days, losing the series 5-0, which became known as a 'blackwash'. I therefore had extra days to tour the island of Barbados and hired a Mini Moke to do so, visiting the usual tourist spots and other interesting places. When it came time to leave, I arrived at Grantly Adams International Airport departures and was directed to the BA's check-in desk for Concorde passengers. After checking in, there was a separate lounge for us to wait in. Shortly, Concorde arrived with incoming passengers, and, once they had disembarked, the aircraft was readied for my flight. However, we were informed that due to repairs being done on the runway at Barbados, the aircraft would not be able to use the full length of runway for take-off. It had therefore only taken on enough fuel to enable the craft to fly as far as the Azores, landing at Santa Maria Airport to refuel for the onward flight to London. This was excellent news as now there would be two take-offs and two landings! In no time at all we were called forward for boarding, so, camera at the ready, I took several pictures before asking a man if he could take a picture of me in front of the waiting Concorde. He duly obliged, and I returned the favour.

My first impression of walking up the steps was how much higher the Concorde was compared to the 747 jumbo on which I had travelled out. Entering the passenger cabin, it was narrow, with two seats either side of the aisle and just 20 rows. My seat was a window number – 6A. Six has always been a significant number in our family: I was married 6 June, Paul was born 6 September, and Mum sadly died 6 October. I found my seat and saw that 6B was already occupied by an elderly lady, who went on to tell me that this was her fourth flight on Concorde. Once all the passengers were on board, the captain's welcome took place, with extra information on what to expect on take-off and what would be happening as the plane went through the sound barrier and reached Mach 2.

I fastened the seatbelt and settled into a very comfy, soft leather seat as the Concorde taxied to the end of the runway. With a roar, the four Rolls Royce Olympus engines thrust the aircraft forward with such power, you were forced back into the seat. Looking out of the window, everything outside was a blur, and, in just a few seconds, the aircraft was airborne, climbing at a very steep rate through some scattered clouds into bright sunshine, levelling out at 45,000ft before climbing to its maximum of 60,000ft. The lady next to me said if I looked out of the window now, I would see the curvature of the earth – we were just on the edge of space. How right she was: what an amazing sight, as, in the distance was this purplish haze and the curve, signifying the edge. I tried to take a photograph but all I got when the film was developed was a picture of myself reflected in the window. (It must have had something to do with the glass used in Concorde's windows.) On the bulkhead at the front for everyone to see was a digital speed counter displaying the air speed. This was watched anxiously by the many passengers who, like me, had never flown on Concorde. In a very short time, the counter registered Mach 1 – 767mph – the speed that sound takes to travel, and we felt a slight bump as the counter registered Mach 2 (1534mph). There is no sensation that signifies you are moving, but by looking out of the window, you can see subsonic aeroplanes like Boeing 747s, 20,000ft below, appearing to go backwards. This is because you are flying almost 800 miles an hour faster than them.

During the two-hour, 20-minute flight whilst on route to the Azores, we were served a champagne dinner of fresh lobster, followed by prime fillet of beef, rum baba with fresh fruit, and coffee. The Azores is a smattering of Portuguese islands in the middle of the Atlantic Ocean, just over halfway on the journey to London. In what seemed no time at all, we were preparing to land at the airport on Santa Maria, the largest island. The descent was very steep compared to a normal aircraft coming into land; the wheels touched at 170mph, and, very quickly, the braking systems slowed Concorde to taxiing speed. Arriving at the terminal, I looked out of the window to see several hundred people waving. This was the first occasion Concorde had landed in the Azores and crowds had come to see this iconic aircraft. For safety reasons, we all left the aircraft and entered the terminal building whilst the plane was refuelled. Inside the terminal building, I was approached by a young boy, who spoke enough English to ask me if I had a photograph of Concorde I could give him. I had to disappoint him but asked him for his name and address, promising to send him one when I arrived home. His name was Ruis. He wrote down his address; I corresponded with him for several years after sending him a postcard of Concorde and other passenger aircraft. He also used the opportunity to practice writing English. It was probably when he became a teenager that we stopped writing to each other, but somewhere in Santa Maria is a man who hopefully kept his Concorde postcard.

There was a slight delay after we got back on board as Concorde had been stopped short of the power plant to restart the engines. Eventually, the problem was solved by a portable power plant, and soon we were taxiing again, ready for take-off. This time, I was ready for the sudden thrust of power and the surge of speed. The word 'exhilarating' does not do the experience justice, and, ever since, I have always fancied a ride in one of the latest RAF F-35 lightning jets.

Climbing up to cruising speed, again at 60,000ft, we were served more champagne and light refreshments. During the journey to London, each passenger was invited into the flight deck to sit beside the flight engineer, who explained the functionality of the aircraft and its capabilities. This would not be permitted today – there are too many safety regulations in place now for passengers to be allowed into the cockpit close to the controls of a plane. A unique feature of Concorde was that as the fuel was used up, the remaining fuel was moved from the front towards the back of the aircraft to maintain the centre of gravity. Just taxiing to the runway for take-off, Concorde burned two tons of fuel, almost 2% of its capacity. In flight, the drooped nose was horizontal, but had to be lowered on landing so the captain could see the runway. We had the flight controls explained by the flight engineer and were introduced to the captain and co-pilot and invited to ask questions. Not everyone took the opportunity to visit the flight deck as there were passengers who had seen it all before!

Settling back into my seat after my turn, I looked out of the window and noticed it had started to get dark as we were now approaching Heathrow and prepared for landing. There was a slight delay as we entered a holding pattern, but Concorde, with its call sign of 'Speedbird', was soon slotted in and the steep descent once again became apparent. Landing perfectly, we disembarked Concorde and went into the terminal building to collect our luggage. Each piece of luggage was tagged with a grey and silver label, the blue and red slash unique to Concorde. I continued to use this on my luggage for some time, until one day it vanished, possibly taken as a souvenir by a baggage handler. It was a while later before I realised I had flown on Concorde – it had not been a dream but a reality, and it had gone all too quickly.

I never got the chance to fly Concorde again, as, on 25 July 2000, an AF Concorde, flight 4590, crashed soon after take-off, killing 100 passengers and nine crew. Concorde flights were grounded whilst an investigation into the crash took place. The subsequent enquiry into the crash revealed that a metallic strip had fallen from a Continental Airline DC-10 that had taken off moments earlier. This metallic strip punctured a tyre on the AF Concorde's left main wheel bogie at take-off. The tyre exploded, and a piece of rubber hit the fuel tank, causing a fuel leak which led to a fire. The crew shut down engine number two in response to the fire warning, and, with engine number one surging and producing little power, the aircraft was unable to gain altitude or speed. The aircraft entered a rapid pitch-up, then a sudden descent, rolling left and crashing into the Hotellissimo Les Relais Bleus Hotel in Gonesse, just outside Paris. The reports into the reason for the crash continue to be disputed to this day, as other well-documented theories have since been shared.

Prior to this crash, Concorde flights had a 100% safety record. Safety improvements were made in the wake of the crash by adding a special lining to protect the fuel tanks, and specially developed burst-resistant tyres were added. After all these modifications, Concorde flew again on 17 July 2001 on a test flight from Heathrow to Iceland, which replicated the London to New York distance. The flight proved a success. The first flight to New York with passengers took place on 11 September 2001, landing shortly before the World Trade Centre attacks. (It was not a commercial flight as all the passengers were BA employees.) Normal commercial operations resumed 7 November 2001 by both BA and AF.

Following the attack on the World Trade Centre, known as 9/11, passenger numbers had declined, so, on 10 April 2003, BA and AF simultaneously announced they would retire their Concordes later that year, citing low passenger numbers and the crash in 2000 as the reason. In a week of farewell flights around the UK, in October

2003, Concorde visited Birmingham, Belfast, Manchester, Cardiff, and Edinburgh. Each day, the aircraft made a return flight out and back into Heathrow, often flying over the cities at low altitude. I was in Carlisle on the morning of 24 October when I heard on the car radio that Concorde had flown into Edinburgh. I abandoned my plans for the day and drove north, stopping at home to collect my camera, before arriving in Edinburgh in time to see this wonderful aircraft soar into the skies for the last time.

It is quite easy to view aircraft taking off from Edinburgh Airport as it is adjacent to the Ingliston Showground which runs parallel to the runway, albeit surrounded by a high security fence. I drove to the runway end and parked up, along with hundreds of other farewell fans. There were enthusiasts with shortwave radios listening to conversations from the control tower. Eventually, the all-clear was given for Concorde to taxi. It stood at the north end of runway one for several minutes before the control tower announced "Speedbird, go!" It began its run, and, with a roar, swept past me and soared like a giant bird into the sky for the last time. I just managed to get a photo as it disappeared within seconds. I felt very emotional as I returned to my car; I sat for several minutes remembering my flight on such a feat of engineering and achievement, enabling ordinary people like me to travel faster than the speed of sound. Of the 20 Concordes built, 18 are still in existence, no longer with an air-worthy certificate but at various museums around the world. One such museum is the National Museum of Flight at East Fortune Airfield, just outside Edinburgh. Visiting it with two of my grandchildren a few years ago, I found inside one of the hangars Concorde G-BOAA. I climbed the steps and sat in seat 6A, closed my eyes, and remembered my flight in 1986. I would love to think it was the same aircraft. Despite some research from old photographs and flight memorabilia of that day, I have so far been unable to ascertain if it was the same one. Meanwhile, as I continue my quest, I like to think Concorde G-BOAA has followed me home to settle in Scotland.

As I type this there is a social media campaign to bring back Concorde. It has the support of thousands, but as much as we all hope it could happen, realistically it is unlikely. Many modifications would have to be made on what was an aircraft of its time; plus, there are now sensitive environmental issues on noise levels and CO_2 emissions.

I was in the right place at the right time, and was very privileged to have travelled faster than the speed of a bullet!

26

LONDON MARATHON

Running and completing the London Marathon had been on my
to-do list ever since the inaugural event on 29 March 1981. It
was founded by athletes Chris Brasher and John Disley, both former
Olympian runners. I was spurred on when Michaela first ran it in 1990.
However, it was not until the autumn of 1992 that I decided I would
apply for a place in April 1993 – the year of my fiftieth. Michaela said
she would do it again and Graham also said he would apply.

Michaela, as a previous runner and elite female athlete, would
automatically have a place, but the only way Graham and I would get
a place was by running for a charity. Michaela heard that Tusk Force,
a charity for the protection of rhinos and elephants, had some vacant
places, so we both applied and guaranteed to raise £1,000 each for
the charity through sponsorship. 68,000 people had applied for the
event that year, the thirteenth time it had taken place. Sponsored by
Nutrasweet, an energy drink, 35,820 had their application accepted,
amongst them Graham and me.

To run any marathon requires a lot of training months before,
so, immediately after Christmas 1992, with the help of Michaela I
embarked on a schedule. This meant taking time out of my working
day, and training during the evenings. As I started the programme, I
wondered whether my left knee would stand up to the hard running

on roads and pavements as it was already giving me some slight pain. (This was the same knee on which I had had keyhole surgery to remove a torn cartilage in 1978.) However, I persisted and religiously stuck to the training schedule. By early February I was beginning to feel good, and the knee was not getting any worse, so, in March, I entered the Alloa half marathon to see what sort of a time I would get, as well as assess my knee. This half marathon is run along the road at the base of the Ochil Hills, known as the 'hillfoots', and, though undulating, there are not too many steep inclines. My time was just under two hours, which was very encouraging, so, all was on course for London.

Michaela was living in North London at the time, so Graham and I flew down to the Capital with British Airways the evening before – Saturday, 17 April 1993 – to stay with her and her husband, George. After feasting on the pasta and jacket potatoes Michaela had cooked for dinner, I went to bed early as we needed to be at the start promptly the next day. A taped rendition of Vengalis's 'Chariots of Fire' was playing in the car as we drove to the station to catch the train to the starting point.

Arriving at the start, runners had to assemble under their numbered block according to what time each runner had estimated their finishing time to be. I had estimated mine to be around four hours. Taking on plenty of water is essential, but it also makes you want to go to the toilet; the queue for the facilities was an obstacle I had to negotiate so I would be comfortable at the start.

As the time counted down to the start for the 25,000 runners who had turned up (10,820 had either pulled out or decided not to run), I found my starting block and waited for the starting gun. Once the gun had sounded, I found that due to the number of runners, it was several minutes before I moved, and then only at a slow walk. Eventually I started to jog over the start line, started my watch to keep timing each mile, and chose to run on the outside of the group. My first mile was just over six minutes. I decided to slow down so that I was averaging seven and a half minutes, a speed I knew I could maintain for the whole race. The next five miles I kept up this pace quite comfortably. Along the route the water stations were frequent, so I grabbed a bottle at each one, ensuring I kept hydrated. I was beginning to enjoy the experience.

Running over Tower Bridge was amazing as you could look down and see the faster runners going through on the cobbles past the Tower of London. It was at this point my running partner, who had been complaining of a problem with his leg, decided to drop out (one of 515 who did not finish). He wished me well and on I went, with each mile now taking me nine minutes. The Isle of Dogs was the toughest part of the course with very few spectators and a stiffish breeze. It was at the 20-mile stage that I started to experience what is known as 'hitting the wall' – a complete loss of energy and weary legs – but I kept going, sometimes jogging, sometimes walking. Michaela had warned me that once I reached 20 miles, I needed as much energy again to finish the last 6.22 miles. I accepted sugary drinks and sweets from the crowd who had turned out to support the race. Spurred on by their support, I gradually felt some strength return and started to jog again rather than walk. Along the Embankment I knew there was only a couple of miles left. Next came Parliament Square, Birdcage Walk, then round in front of Buckingham Palace, on to Westminster Bridge and the finish line, the Houses of Parliament and Big Ben in the background.

Approaching the bridge, I suddenly felt euphoric and sprinted the last 100 yards, overtaking several runners. My time shown on the finish line photograph was just over five hours, but it had taken me over 10 minutes to get to the start line. I was therefore happy with my time of under five hours. Graham's time was under four, Michaela's under three.

Delighted with our medals, we had a joint picture together before saying goodbye to Michaela as Graham and I returned to the airport to fly back to Scotland. Boarding the flight with the medals around our necks, we received warm applause from the passengers who had already boarded.

We both succeeded in raising more than the £1,000 each for the Tusk Force Charity.

Having got a taste for running, as I was now very fit and with no after effects apart from a bruised right toenail (which to this day doesn't grow properly), I entered several more half marathons in Alloa, Glasgow, Stirling, and Edinburgh, as well as some 10km races, one of which was the Balmoral, the former Queen's Scottish country residence, which I ran with my-daughter-in law, Nicola. However, I did not do any more full marathons as my knee again became troublesome, later resulting in more keyhole surgery to remove torn cartilage.

27

MUNROIST

In July 1977, we embarked on a touring caravan holiday to Scotland. Kate and I had been to Scotland in 1962 before we were married, staying at a Butlin's holiday camp in Ayr, taking two days to get there in my Austin 8. Now we had a Vauxhall estate, towing a Sprite Alpine caravan with two children: Michaela, aged eleven, and Graham, aged eight. Kate was seven months pregnant with Paul.

We toured along the west side of Loch Lomond and stopped for lunch in a layby opposite the Loch Sloy power station on the A82. Directly across Loch Lomond on the opposite side of the water was a prominent-looking mountain that I learned was Ben Lomond. Looking at it from a distance, you could see people on the summit who looked the size of matchsticks. Whilst having lunch, I periodically watched the scene for about an hour: people were continually coming and going, so it was obvious this mountain was popular, and climbable. Deciding that it was something we could do, a day later we drove along the road on the east bank of Loch Lomond and parked in the Rowardennan Forest car park where the track led out of the forest to the flanks of the mountain. Taking food and drink in a Tupperware box in a string bag, we left Kate in the caravan and started the walk. The weather was sunny, with scattered cloud as we followed the track towards the summit. Out on the flanks, the views across Loch Lomond were spectacular as all the various islands in the loch came into view. I cannot remember how long it took us, but we reached the summit trig point and had a 360-degree view of Scotland. This was my first Munro, Michaela and Graham's too. We did not know it then, but all mountains in Scotland over 3,000ft (914 metres) are known as Munros after they were logged by Sir Hugh Munro in 1891. The original list consisted of 283 separate mountains, over 3,000ft in height. In 1977, after several revisions by the Scottish Mountaineering Club, there were 286, and we had just 'bagged' our first. ('Bagging Munros' became popular from the late 1960s and those who finished them become known as 'Compleaters'.)

A few days later, we had moved on and found ourselves in a campsite outside Fort William. We were in Glen Nevis, with another mountain towering above us. The mountain was Ben Nevis, Britain's highest mountain at 4,413ft (1345 metres). People were returning to the campsite and talking about having climbed it, so we thought we would also attempt it. We had to wait a couple of days as the weather was wet and miserable, but, eventually, we had a clear day. We set out after breakfast with sandwiches and drink in the same Tupperware box and string bag. We wore plimsoles – this was in the days before walking boots and trainers. We crossed a bridge over the River Nevis and picked up what has since become known as 'The Tourist Path'. It was an easy path to follow – as we got higher and higher, we could look back at where the caravan was parked – and we started taking pictures with Kate's 35mm slide camera. After about an hour, an elderly gentleman stopped us on his way down and spoke to Michaela and Graham. He handed them a piece of paper with handwritten details of what summits could be seen from the top. Telling us to be careful with the footwear we were wearing, he then went on his way. It was not until many years later that I came to realise the old gentleman was Alfred Wainwright who went on to write many guidebooks on the fells of the Lake District, as well as books on Scotland's mountains.

It was three-and-a-half hours later before we approached the final climb towards the summit, a gully still covered in deep snow! Arriving at the top in glorious sunshine, we studied the piece of paper we had been given and tried to pick out the various Munro summits all around. We had conquered Britain's highest mountain and 'bagged' our second Munro. We returned down the same path, which was quite steep, in about half the time it took to climb up. Waiting back at the caravan, Kate had prepared dinner which was very welcome after such a long day out.

It was whilst working for Barclays Life that I was introduced to the TRIMARC club – The Rock Ice Mountaineering and Rambling Club. This club had been formed in the 1970s, the early members being Ray Cade, David Levy, Trevor Boothby, Tony Catley, and Stuart Hodgson, who all worked for Barclays Bank in one capacity or another. As a family, we had become members whilst living in Newmarket as the club organised family walks, as well as more strenuous days away, every spring and autumn. The spring and autumn trips were more of an expedition, with serious mountains to climb. These would be organised in the Lake District or Wales, whatever the weather. We would drive overnight on a Friday from Newmarket to the location and then climb mountains on the Saturday and Sunday, before driving back home. October and November were usually the choice for the Lakes as it meant snow conditions. Sometimes the snow conditions were so bad that just getting there was difficult, as I found out on one occasion when trying to cross the A66 near Bowes Moor with Rodney Wright, a colleague and friend. There had been so much snow that the road upon which we were driving was completely blocked, with snowdrifts covering lorries. We were turned back by the police roadblock. To get to the Lakes, we had to head further north on the A1 and then cut across country on the A69 just outside Newcastle, then go south down the A6/M6.

The first such trip was led by Stuart Hodgson on 2 and 3 December 1977, when we climbed three Wainwrights (as the hills are known) in the Lake District: Helvellyn, Nethermost Pike, and Grisdale Pike.

These trips continued until we moved to Scotland in 1980. From The Arns, two Munros were visible across the fields: Ben Vorlich at 985 metres, and Stùc a' Chròin at 975 metres. For three days in 1981, we housed six members of TRIMARC at The Arns and everyone succeeded in climbing both. It was during this occasion that Graham, then aged 15, joined us. He caught the bug and started to tick off more Munros thereafter.

Members of TRIMARC then made frequent visits to Scotland to help Graham complete the list, usually in October and April of each year. Sometimes we would break the mould and visit the Hebridean Islands. Friendships with Ray, David and Trevor became ever stronger as we all had the same desire of conquering hills, whether in the Lake District, Wales or Scotland. In between these meets, Graham and I would plan midweek trips. One such trip was to Skye on 26 and 27 June 1995 when we based ourselves at the Sligachan Hotel to climb the Sligachan Munros: Sgurr nan Gillean, Am Basteir, and Bruach na Frithe. Despite the snow lying in the upper gullies, the day became extremely hot; by the time we reached the summit of Sgurr nan Gillean, the temperature was over 90 degrees Fahrenheit. The view from the summit was incredible, and, in the Scottish Mountaineering Club Hillwalker's Guidebook, it is described as one of the world's greatest mountain views. It was a memorable day, captured on video. (I remember carrying one of our first video cameras which was quite heavy.) Another memory of that day is plunging into a lovely pool of water beneath a waterfall to cool off on the walk back to the hotel. Not having any swimwear, we just stripped off and jumped in. Upon climbing back out, we were soon covered in hordes of infamous Scottish midges.

This was the start of regular visits to Skye to tick off the 11 Munros. The ridges on Skye are almost alpine-like and are unlike any other Munro. One such Munro, known as 'The Inaccessible Pinnacle', requires rock climbing skills, so we hired a guide who taught us how to abseil, using a rowan tree in his garden before then graduating to sea cliffs, and then finally tackling The Inaccessible Pinnacle. Paul accompanied us on this trip. Graham and the guide climbed up and along the east ridge of the Munro using pitches, whilst Paul and I waited on the west side. Once at the summit, the guide lowered a rope attached to a fixed point on the top. We then attached the rope to the climbing harness we were wearing and climbed up the wall of the west face. Paul went first and I have never seen him move so quickly to get to the top. He said afterwards that he just wanted to get it over with as there was a drop of over 2,000ft to the bottom!

In 2002, Graham became the first member of the family, and of TRIMARC, to complete the Munros: on Buchaille Stob na Bròige in Glencoe (Munroist no. 3982).

I had accompanied Graham on many trips, usually the most difficult ones involving ridges where it was not sensible for him to go on his own. Many times, we left in the early hours, when the weather forecast was favourable, to tick off whatever he had worked out was possible to do in one day. As the closer daytrip Munros were completed, we had to plan to travel farther afield. On several occasions I would finish playing cricket on a Saturday, collect Graham, and then we would head north to a B&B in readiness to climb the next day. We had some fantastic days together, sometimes accompanied by Paul who by then had also got the bug.

It was after Graham's last Munro, Buachaille Etive Mor, that David Levy said to me:

"You've done a fair number of the Munros with Graham and probably most of the difficult ones – why don't you try to do them all?"

This seemed a great suggestion and was made even more plausible by David saying that he would make regular trips every five weeks or so up to Scotland to accompany me. I had not kept a comprehensive list of the Munros I had done, but Graham and David had. From their records it was easy to work out what I still had to do to be 'a compleater'.

So began my quest, with David's regular trips throughout the year, as well as Graham finding time off work between David's trips to help me. This meant my son was doing several of them for the second time, but he did not mind. The autumn and spring TRIMARC trips also revolved around me finishing the Munros, my personal target to finish them before my seventieth birthday. This deadline, however, got pushed back by six months when on a trip in June 2009 with David and Graham into Wester Ross to climb four Munros in Fisherfield, we got stranded on the wrong side of the river Abhainn Strath na Sealga from our camp. I damaged my right knee after several attempts to cross the river which had swollen with heavy rain all day. Eventually, at 10pm, we decided we would have to spend the night on the opposite riverbank and try to find shelter. David had made it across an hour earlier as he had turned back after deciding not to do the third and fourth Munros. Fortunately, Graham had a striker that enabled us to light some toilet paper to start a fire, to which we added dry, dead gorse and dry, dead wood so that we could build a fire. (Without the fire we would have been in trouble as we were both soaked through from the all-day rain). We sheltered under my survival sheet the best we could, drying our clothes by the fire and monitoring the river until at last it stopped raining at around 4am and we heard a cuckoo. It was not until 8.30am that the river had subsided sufficiently for us to wade across to our tents and meet up with David for breakfast. We had survived on the few snacks during the night that we had left over from the day before. After having some breakfast, we packed up our tents to walk out. I found it difficult with my knee but eventually made it back to the car. However, my knee was so severely damaged that an operation was inevitable. The operation to repair the knee was carried out in early September but it took six months of recovery before the knee was strong enough again. I went on the autumn trip to Glen Shiel in October, but I had to be content to do things tourists do whilst the TRIMARC group climbed the hills.

It was on 25 July 2013, accompanied by 27 friends and family members, when I became the family's second Munroist (Munroist no. 5289) when I stood on top of Beinn na Lap at 937 metres, a bottle of champagne and the traditional malt whisky to celebrate.

This Munro is unique as the access requires a journey on the highland trainline to Britain's highest railway station, Corrour, and, from there, walking to the summit. We all descended, returning to Corrour Station to find a parcel that had been left for the attention of Mike Nash. Upon opening it, I discovered a case of specially labelled bottles of real ale called Mike Nash's Last Munro Ale. What a surprise, organised by Graham. Everyone duly took a bottle and toasted my success.

On the train journey back to the Bridge of Orchy, my granddaughter, Rachael, told the train conductor that I had climbed all the Munros, so he announced it over the passenger intercom. This led to a huge round of applause by everyone on the train. Back at the hotel, everyone got changed, ready for the private dinner organised with the Bridge of Orchy Hotel where we had booked in for the evening. An engraved glass plaque was presented to me, suitably engraved with the profile of Beinn na Lap, plus a map of the Munros, on the back of which were the signatures of everyone who had accompanied me on the final summit. My friends from Australia, Fred and Julia, had sent two bottles of fine wine which were presented to me as an acknowledgement from the other side of the world. It really was a momentous day that I will never forget.

28

MY BATTLE WITH
TRIGEMINAL NEURALGIA

This account first begins in September 2006, when I felt a sudden pain in my lower left jaw whilst on a river cruise from St Petersburgh to Moscow with Kate. When I returned, I went to see my dentist, who, though could find nothing wrong with my teeth, prescribed antibiotics as he thought I might have an infection. The course of antibiotics made no difference; I continued to experience sudden, sharp attacks of pain, particularly when eating or speaking. After experiencing this pain intermittently for about two weeks, I made an appointment to see my GP. He suggested I see an oral specialist at the local hospital and made me an appointment for the following week.

The oral specialist arranged for a scan of my mouth and jaw. The results showed no gross abnormality, the findings summarised as: 'No definite cause for the patient's symptoms as demonstrated on this examination'. The specialist, however, prescribed Carbamazepine to relieve the pain. Returning home, Kate decided to research mouth pain on the Internet and suggested I had trigeminal neuralgia (TN), which was described online as 'the most excruciating pain known to man and has no known cure'. She told me that the drug I had been prescribed was apparently the best available for the condition. I have never liked taking drugs, not even for a headache, so I did not take the Carbamazepine straightaway, hoping the pain would clear up on its own. However, this did not happen; now, the excruciating pain had started to not only affect my ability to eat, drink and speak, but also to shave. It got so bad that I started taking the Carbamazepine, and, after a few days, the drug did suppress the symptoms. Then, after about three months, the pain suddenly subsided and I stopped taking it.

The pain returned six months later, only to then go into remission for several weeks before returning. The cycle continued, and each time the pain intensity was stronger. I continued like this for the next four years until Carbamazepine no longer worked. It was also causing me to have a very irregular heart rhythm. My GP then prescribed Tegretol which, for a time, gave better results. I also tried to manage the pain but found it was affecting my way of life, so, in desperation, I returned to my GP who referred me to a consultant neurologist in Edinburgh. After the consultation, the neurosurgeon confirmed the diagnosis as idiopathic trigeminal neuralgia. His suggestion was to keep trying different drugs – Oxcarbazepine, Pregabalin, Phenytoin. He also suggested a form of surgery, performed by his consultant neurosurgeon colleague, Patrick Statham.

In May 2011, I saw Mr Statham privately at Spire Murrayfield Hospital in Edinburgh and he sent me for an MRI scan. This revealed that there was a small vessel – a branch of the anterior inferior cerebella artery – tickling the insertion of the left trigeminal nerve into the pons. He described my options. One was continuing with medication, trying different anticonvulsants. Another was having injections with Glycerol, which may have to be repeated, or surgery muscular decompression which was likely to be the most successful (it had a 10% chance of recurrence afterwards). He also explained a surgical procedure that would involve drilling into the skull just behind the left ear to expose the area and separate the nerve which was trapped between two blood vessels. The risk of death, stroke, hearing loss, CSF leaks, and meningitis were clearly explained. I decided to continue with medication for the time being, as the periods of remission made the condition manageable. I was accustomed to hospitals, what with the previous surgeries I'd undertaken, all sports-related – hernia, knees, shoulder, and legs – but I was never keen on them, even as a visitor, so decided against the surgical option at that point. I continued taking Tegretol whenever needed.

It was three years later, when I was at the Commonwealth Games in Glasgow 2014, that the pain returned after being in remission for several weeks; so severe, I resorted to the Tegretol once again. This time there was no more remission. I tolerated this by taking increasing amounts of the drug, until it was over 200mg a day. I was suffering abnormal heart rhythms again, as well as double vision. I clearly remember looking at the train departure board at Edinburgh Waverley Station whilst trying to get home, everything a blur.

On holiday in Madeira in November 2014, the high dosage of Tegretol caused me to fall over with dizzy spells and double vision. One evening, I was helped back to our apartment by holding onto my wife. To anyone watching, they must have thought she was escorting a drunk; I was stumbling all over the place due to the amount of Tegretol I was now having to take. This episode prompted me to see Mr Statham again when I returned home.

I made an appointment just before Christmas 2014 and explained my symptoms and how the pain had intensified. After another MRI scan, Mr Statham once again explained the options. He did, however, point out that if I left it much longer, he could not conduct the procedure due to my age (I was 71). He described the surgery again and said that there was a video clip online I could watch to see what the operation entailed. Though not trying to persuade me to have it done, he did emphasise that I was fit and healthy, both in my favour. After discussing it all at length again with Kate, I watched the video and decided to have the operation.

I telephoned Mr Statham's secretary immediately after Christmas and said I wanted to proceed. Although I was to be admitted as a private patient to the Spire Murrayfield Hospital in Edinburgh (thanks to my healthcare policy), I had to wait until 3 March 2015 before I could be admitted to the Edinburgh Western General Infirmary where Mr Statham was the leading neurosurgeon. (The Western General had the specialist equipment needed for the operation.) During the intervening weeks, I was desperately hoping that no serious emergency arose that would prevent the operation from being delayed, as I had been informed that as the lead neurosurgeon, Mr Statham may have to prioritise another patient in such a situation.

Though I was not keen on hospitals, on the morning of the operation the pain was so bad, I really did not care. I was now taking warfarin to thin my blood as the irregular heart rhythms caused by Tegretol could, my GP said, cause a stroke. I had to stop the warfarin five days before being admitted but continued taking Tegretol for the pain. As I woke on the morning of 3 March 2015, fog, snow, and ice were everywhere. However, Graham, who lives in Edinburgh, drove to Dunblane to collect me. I was having another bout of TN as we drove towards the Western General Hospital. Kate was with me, so too Graham, and I was quite relieved when I registered to be given a surgical gown and surgical stockings in readiness for theatre. Basic checks were conducted as I waited with Kate in a precheck cubicle. At 10am, I was taken into theatre and introduced to the team of anaesthetists and other technicians who were going to be looking after me, monitoring blood pressure, heart rate, oxygen levels, and so on. There seemed to be so many of them that I became quite mesmerised by all the attention. Once I was connected to all the monitors, I was given the anaesthetic injection to put me to sleep.

Four hours later, I woke up in the intensive care unit, connected to various leads, an oxygen mask over my face. One of the intensive care nurses removed the mask and offered me a drink through a straw. After taking a sip, I started to take in my surroundings and realised I was free of pain. An hour later, Kate and Paul came to visit me, though I barely knew they were there. I had a morphine pump which I controlled by squeezing if I experienced pain from the surgery; I remember little else. I was in the intensive care ward for two days before being transferred to a room with three other patients. I was discharged a week later. Mr Statham checked on me every day for any signs of complications with hearing, eyesight, and face numbness; thankfully there were none. I had a large scar behind my left ear running down to my neck, 18 staples holding the wound together. The staples were removed on the day of discharge. I thanked the staff of the Edinburgh Western General; I could not have been looked after any better – the care was excellent.

For over four weeks afterwards, I took strong painkillers for headaches. I also suffered from nausea and lost my appetite during this time. My lovely wife cared for me during my recovery and told me that she became very emotional when I went into the theatre, thinking I would not survive the operation. After six weeks, I returned to see Mr Statham who again checked all my functions: hearing, speech, and sensitivity to the face. He took me through the procedure in detail and showed me on a computer screen exactly where the nerve was trapped between the blood vessels. He said it was exactly how they had seen it on the MRI scan, and, though it had been very tricky to tickle it out without damaging major blood vessels, the operation went perfectly. (I now have a Teflon-type pad separating the nerve from the blood vessels in my head.) For three months following the operation I felt very tired and lacked energy, before I started to feel well enough to do some light gardening tasks. It was almost six months before I was back to normal fitness, and, after the next checkup with Mr Statham in September, he discharged me. I mentioned that the worst part was the recurring headaches for the first two months to which he said, "The brain doesn't like being interfered with."

It is now 10 years since the operation; eight years since I received a telephone call from Edinburgh Western General Hospital, asking if I would answer some questions as they were doing a review of the TN procedures. I was more than happy to provide my feedback; I will for ever be grateful for the surgical skills of Mr Statham and his team. Mr Statham gave his permission for me to send a copy of this text to the Trigeminal Neuralgia Association of which I have been a member now for many years. The Association published my story a few months later in their quarterly magazine, so I hope that other people suffering this awful condition are benefitting from my experience.

I was pleased that the operation was such a success as I have had no further TN problems since. The condition only affects 1 in 10,000, and, as such, receives little funding for research. I continue to support the Trigeminal Neuralgia Association, making it my number one charity.

29

LONG-DISTANCE WALKS

A TV programme called On the West Highland Way presented by Jimmy MacGregor, a Scottish folk singer and journalist, was shown over several episodes in 1986. The West Highland Way is a long-distance walk from Milngavie, just north of Glasgow, to Fort William, a total of 96 miles. The trail was opened in 1980 and was Scotland's first officially designated long-distance route. It is now recognised by Nature Scotland as one of Scotland's great trails.

I discussed with Graham, then aged 17, the possibility of walking the West Highland Way with him. He agreed, and I started researching places we could stop to rest at the end of each day. I then mentioned it to my salespeople at Target Life, surprised when John Doherty, who lived in Fort William, said he was keen to accompany Graham and me. In fact, such was the interest that we decided to do it as a sponsored walk in aid of Cancer Research UK, a disease that Mum died of at only 62, and Dad at 74. Working through a guidebook and map produced on the back of the TV series, I started booking B&Bs and small hotels for the three of us. Once we had all the accommodation in place, we started looking for sponsorship.

On 13 June 1987, Graham and I met John at Milngavie railway station, the starting point. We posed for a photograph on the board that announced the start and set off. The walk initially passed through a busy shopping precinct before emerging into Mugdock Country Park. Leaving the park, we then joined an old disused railway track, originally built in 1867 to link Killearn to Glasgow. We reached the village of Drymen and then proceeded up Conic Hill, with fantastic views of Loch Lomond, before descending into Balmaha. By then we had completed the first 20 miles. It was now early evening, so we found the B&B I had booked, checked in, then went to the local pub for dinner. We went to sleep the first night feeling pleased with ourselves.

After breakfast the next morning, we left just after 9am, following the trail through ancient oak woodland which had been planted for shipbuilding centuries before. We paused for some lunch at Rowardennan, where, in 1977, I had parked the caravan whilst climbing Ben Lomond with Michaela and Graham. The next stop was Inveranan, 21 miles distant, but, due to the difficult walking terrain on the east bank of Loch Lomond, we lost time; we were never going to reach the point from where you raise a flag for the hotel to send a boat over from Ardlui, on the west side, to collect you. Instead, we arrived at Inversnaid, a shortfall of six miles. With the wet weather, I entered the Inversnaid Hotel and enquired at reception if they had two rooms for the night. Fortunately, they did.

The next morning the rain had cleared, and we proceeded further along the east side of Loch Lomond where the terrain was easier, heading for Crainlarich 12 miles away – the next overnight stay. The B&B at Crainlarich was very comfortable, and, after checking in, we wandered down to the local pub called the Rod and Eel for something to eat. My memory of that evening is of Graham taking on the locals at pool and winning every game!

We had breakfast early the following morning then set off, leaving Crainlarich behind. The next overnight stay was scheduled at a hotel at Bridge of Orchy, 12 miles away. We made good progress to Tyndrum through woodland forest paths, then into an area that was once a lead mine, the ground still scarred from that activity. It was here that John found the sole had come away from one of his boots. He changed into his golf shoes, which he was carrying, and, at Tyndrum, telephoned his wife Moira and asked her to bring him another pair of boots from Fort William. We stopped for refreshments at the local village shop, had a short rest, then picked up the route towards Bridge of Orchy. For me, this was the most interesting section, as, for a long time, it runs parallel to the West Highland railway line, with a continuous view of Ben Dorain, a Munro. Passing trains sounded their claxon and passengers gave us a wave. We arrived at the Bridge of Orchy Hotel in the late afternoon and checked in at reception. I had managed thus far without any foot problems, but upon removing my boots, saw a blister on my big toe. I filled the bath and decided to lance the blister to ease the pressure. We all had dinner in the bar and enjoyed the chat with other walkers – some also on the West Highland Way, others 'bagging the Munros' – before retiring to bed.

The following morning, after a late breakfast, we set off. Our next stop was Kingshouse Hotel just 13 miles away. This section was wild and remote as we crossed into Rannoch Moor, stunning views of the mountains to the northwest. Most of this section follows the old military road built by General Wade, so the terrain was favourable if a bit undulating. On the highest point is a memorial for Peter Fleming, brother of Ian, author of the James Bond novels. Peter had unfortunately died of a heart attack on Rannoch Moor whilst out stalking deer. We stopped there for a photo and snack, in glorious sunshine. As we descended Buachaille Etive Mòr – the imposing mountain at the head of Glen Coe – came into view. Further on, we passed the White Corries Ski Centre then crossed the main A82 and the path to the Kingshouse Hotel. It was early afternoon, so we checked in and relaxed as the next day would be a tough stretch to Kinlochleven. This section includes the infamous Devil's Staircase, the ascent out of Glen Coe.

Starting early after breakfast the next morning, we made the start of the Devil's Staircase after half an hour which was not as strenuous as its name suggests. The views looking back to Glen Coe and the opposite ridge were amazing and so memorable. We attained the highest point where we had a view of the Blackwater dam and began the descent into Kinlochleven. This village resulted primarily from the construction of an aluminium smelter plant. It was run by a hydro-electric scheme high up in the mountains, powered by the water from the Blackwater dam. The village was the first in the world to have every house connected to electricity; it became known as 'The Electric Village'. I had booked a B&B, so, after locating it, we got changed and wandered down to the local pub for some refreshments. The pub was called The Tailrace, named after the water expended from driving the turbines that power the village. It was a delightful evening.

Next morning, we picked up the West Highland Way again and began our ascent out of Kinlochleven towards our destination, Fort William, 15 miles away. The ascent was harder than the Devil's Staircase as it was quite steep through woodland, meaning we had to avoid exposed tree roots. We eventually emerged from the treeline into the beautiful Larigmore Valley, with a view of the Pap of Glencoe (2,431ft) to the north. We pushed on, stopping for a break at Lundrava; now we had a view of Ben Nevis. The descent into Fort William took us through forestry, until we emerged onto the road and the last mile to the finishing sign. John phoned his wife from the shop nearby to collect us. We stayed overnight at John's and had a delightful meal with his wife, Moria, and young son, Iain.

The following day, we were joined by Jean Band, who had driven up from her dwelling in Larbert to take us back home. First, though, there was the task of finishing the walk. This entailed climbing Ben Nevis to raise the money for Cancer Research UK. Ben Nevis is not part of the West Highland Way but an added challenge afterwards, for which we had received sponsorship. We were accompanied by Moira, Iain, and Jean, who all made it to the top. I was again on Britain's highest mountain with Graham, 10 years after we had both first climbed it with Michaela.

All three of us successfully raised £1,410.

Over 10,000 people now do this long-distance walk every year, a walk that has meant a lot to me and the family since completing the first one.

In June 2011, I accompanied Kate, who wanted to undertake the challenge to raise money for Alzheimer's after her sister's diagnosis and subsequent sad death from the disease. We set off on Sunday 5 June 2011, stopping at different places to those I had used 24 years earlier. Drymen was the first overnight stop – 12 miles. The next day we made it to Rowadennan. It was our 47th wedding anniversary which we celebrated with a bar lunch and stay at the Rowardennan Hotel. The third day was a gruelling distance of 21 miles in driving rain, hail and thunderstorms, but Kate, though not being used to the harsh conditions, coped well. It took 12 hours to finally reach Crainlarich, whereupon our B&B hosts dried all our wet clothes and gave us welcoming cups of tea. We got changed and walked to the Rod & Eel pub for some food. I sent a text to Graham:

'There are guys in here looking for a game of bar billiards!' (My little joke, referring to 1987 when he beat all the locals).

After a good night's sleep, we set off for Bridge of Orchy, 14 miles away, stopping at Tyndrum for a hot lunch at the Green Welly shop. The weather was fine and sunny, so the stretch to Bridge of Orchy was pleasant (especially after the day before), and we were buoyed on by the train drivers hooting and passengers waving from the carriages. We reached the hotel late afternoon. After checking in, we rested before dinner.

The following day, it was just 13 miles to Kingshouse, the same location where we had stayed in 1987, as well as when we had enjoyed a celebration dinner on 28 August 2002 when Graham completed all the Munros. It was also here that I realised we were not going to finish until the Saturday. As I had accepted an appointment to umpire a Scottish League match at Penicuik, I called the appointment's secretary to cancel.

We set off from Kingshouse, Kate showing some trepidation about the prospect of Devil's Staircase. However, the morning was fine and sunny, and, in no time, we started to climb up it and out of Glen Coe. Glen Coe was made notorious for its massacre of the MacDonalds by government forces, for failing to pledge allegiance to the new monarchs, William III and Mary II, during the Jacobite rising. Upon reaching the highest point, the view looking back was breathtaking, a vista of mountains all around. As we descended, more walkers and runners started to appear, having started from Kinlochleven. We later learned that the Royal Bank of Scotland had organised a charity walk that day called The Walk of Your Life, so 800 participants, some in outlandish costumes, passed us as we descended to Kinlochleven. In Kinlochleven is an interesting museum, documenting the story of the aluminium plant and the building of the dam by Irish workers, many of whom died and are now buried in a graveyard near the dam.

We both felt fine, ready for the final leg, 14 miles to Fort William, where resident John Doherty was to meet us. The climb out of the village is steep, the path through woodland, but once through, the walk follows the old military road along the valley floor. Soon the infamous Marmores came into view, where, as part of my Munros challenge, I had climbed The Ring of Steal; this I'd done in winter conditions with Graham, a really scary day using crampons and ice axes. We pushed on to reach Lundavra Farm where an information board pointed to the trail ahead. We stopped for a sandwich and drink before moving on, the path undulating. Soon, the mighty bulk of Ben Nevis came into view, signifying that our walk down into Glen Nevis was almost complete. Following a gravel track down into Glen Nevis, we emerged on to the road and started the walk to the finish. After only 10 minutes, a car pulled up and asked if we wanted a lift. It was John Doherty. We obviously declined his offer, which was made in jest, finally arriving

15 minutes later at the board announcing the finish. Photo taken, we then proceeded to accept the lift to John's house, where we were met by Moira and welcoming cups of tea.

The next day, we caught the Highland train back home, often passing parts of our walk in the opposite direction. Kate raised £1500 for Alzheimer's Research, and I had enjoyed the walk for the second time with my wife, which would remain special on the week of our 47th anniversary!

10 days later, Graham ran the whole distance in under 24 hours whilst taking part in the annual ultra race.

10 years later, in 2021, following the loss of Kate to a stroke in July 2020, Michaela, Graham and Paul decided to run the distance in their mum's memory and raise money for Stroke Research. They were supported with a backup team of all the family, plus Tom Liddell. It was a mammoth undertaking for which they all trained for over six months. They set off at 10pm on 28 May, finishing in the centre of Fort William a few minutes after the 24-hour target they had set themselves. (The finish had now been moved to the town centre, away from the original finishing place.) Through the support of family, friends and many unknown donors, they raised more than £7,000 for Stroke Research. Their mum would have been so proud, as was I.

Jimmy MacGregor, the presenter of the 1986 West Highland Way series, made another programme, this time on Scotland's longest coast to coast walk – The Southern Upland Way – 214 miles, opened since his original TV series. The walk runs from Portpatrick on the Atlantic coast to Cove on the North Sea, finishing at Cockburnspath, a much more demanding walk with a total elevation of 25,509ft.

Deciding to undertake the challenge with Graham, we planned the overnight stops again, supporting small hotels and B&Bs. The night before we set off, we travelled to Portpatrick, staying at the Portpatrick Hotel ready for setting off on 21 April 1992. This time I had a Nokia

1011 mobile phone (the size of a small pouch) and a spare battery. Our first day was 23 miles to New Luce where we stayed in the local pub and learned from the locals all about how they hunted foxes by 'lamping'. The distance to cover on the next day was 17.5 miles, to Bargrennan, known for its prehistoric, chambered cairns. This was followed by a day spent walking 24 miles to St. Johns Town of Dalry, a very old town that grew primarily by servicing the needs of pilgrims travelling from Edinburgh to the nearby church at Whithorn, established by St. Ninian. By now my heels were getting badly blistered. (This was the days before Gore-Tex footwear, so my heavy leather boots never properly dried out.) It was a relief to reach each destination, take off my boots, and swaddle my feet in cotton wool and plasters. The next morning was sheer agony when I started to walk, until the blisters broke open again. At the end of every day, once we had stopped at the overnight stay and had washed, Graham, the saviour, dressed my raw heels.

The distance to Carspairn, the next point, was 15 miles through forests, making navigation difficult. However, we made it to a remote farmhouse where I had booked dinner, bed and breakfast. The lady welcomed us with a beer after taking our wet clothes to dry. We got changed and were presented with a traditional farmhouse meal which was most welcome after the day we had had. We enjoyed a couple of beers from our host beside a big open fire before going to bed.

It was 20 miles to our next destination – Warnlochead. It rained as we left our comfortable farmhouse and it did not relent for the whole day, but we managed to find an abandoned chicken coop to squeeze into and stop briefly for a bite to eat; it was a relief to escape the rain. Firstly, through farmland then forest, we made it to the second highest summit on the route, Benbrack (581 metres). It was when we descended again into forestry that Graham started to have problems with his Achilles. We kept stopping to rest, Graham convinced he needed to buy a pair of soft trainers at the approaching village of Sanquhar. We made Sanquhar around midday, the village noted for its tiny post office established in 1712 and considered the oldest working establishment in the world. Graham succeeded in purchasing a pair of trainers in another local store, changed into them, and felt more comfortable as we picked up the route towards Warnlochead. Warnlochead, an old mining village, is the highest in Scotland, standing at 425 metres. It was established in the Middle Ages when lead was discovered in the surrounding hills and was mined until the 1950s. It was almost dark by the time we descended into the valley of Warnlochhead, passing abandoned mine equipment, including a narrow-gauge railway track. Soaked through, we found our B&B. Once again, we were welcomed by the host to whom we handed our wet clothes and shown where to bathe, ready for dinner. Our host, who had to visit her mother, left us breakfast, which we ate before we set off again.

From the village, a large golf ball-structure was obvious on the hill ahead. This was Lowther Hill, the highest point on the route at 710 metres and our first objective, the Way passing over the summit. (The 'golf ball' hides a radar station used by NATS.) Ascending to the top so early after breakfast was strenuous but the views were amazing, giving a panoramic view of all the surrounding hills. This day entailed a 20-mile walk to Beattock from where we were to be met by Trevor Boothby, a long-term friend of ours from TRIMARC. We made good time as the weather had improved, and, by late afternoon, we could hear the traffic from the busy A74 which passes by Beattock. Soon, the village appeared below as we came to the top of rising ground. I had once been forced to stay overnight in the Beattock Hotel due to bad weather when I commuted to Scotland from Poynton in 1981. This was my first time back. We checked in to a different hotel and were just going to the room when Trevor arrived. We had a beer together, after which we changed and arranged a time for dinner. Over dinner we chatted about our journey so far and caught up with Trevor's news.

The following morning, we set off after having breakfast together, crossing under the busy A74 (now the M74) towards Moffat, the next village. Our final destination, however, was 21 miles away – St. Mary's Loch. Trevor would accompany us until it was time for him to return to Beattock and the drive back to Solihull, where he lived. The weather was overcast but we made good progress as we passed through Moffat into the Moffat hills. At Ettrich Head, the border between Dumfries and Galloway and the Scottish Borders, Trevor decided to head back to Beattock for his drive home. At this point, every drop of water that falls behind you flows into the Atlantic, and every drop in front flows into the North Sea. In the instant that we said goodbye to Trevor and thanked him for his company, the rain started. We watched as he descended into the valley until he was out of sight. We later learned that he had had a very wet walk back to his car and an even wetter journey home. We pushed on, and, by late afternoon, started the climb up and over to St. Mary's Loch. We descended between St. Mary's Loch and the smaller Loch of the Lowes and sighted the Tibbie Shiels Inn, our home for the night. The old coaching inn was established in 1823 by Isabella 'Tibbie' Shiels who started taking in lodgers after her husband, a mole catcher, died soon after they moved there. Over the years she had extended the cottage. It is now a pub that provides accommodation. We checked in and spent a very enjoyable evening in the bar, drinking and eating, and chatting with the locals before retiring to bed.

The next morning, we calculated that we had just over 70 miles to go to reach the finish at Cockburnspath, so were now well over halfway. My heels were still needing to be patched up before we set off. The route was 12 miles to Traquair, the village for our overnight stop. The path from the inn follows the edge of St. Mary's Loch for about three miles, so it was very pleasant walking, and the weather, though overcast, was fine. Leaving the loch behind and walking an ascent of no more than 360 metres, we made good time to reach our overnight stay which was some distance off the route. Traquair is a small village, famous for Scotland's oldest inhabited property, Traquair House. Having checked in, before dinner Graham went shopping for more food supplies and padding for my heels.

The following day, our hosts offered to drive us back to where we had left the route, thus offering me the chance to avoid enduring the discomfort of the extra distance until my heels got used to moving again, which was appreciated. This day would be an 18-mile walk to Melrose. Initially, we climbed through moorland and woodland before emerging onto more wild moorland, the Three Brethren in the distance. These are large cairns visible for miles around and represent the meeting point of three large Scottish estates. Pausing for a photo and a bite to eat before descending through more woodland, we then crossed a bridge over the River Tweed and through more farmland before arriving in Galashiels. Stopping briefly in Galashiels, we then followed the path by the river, pausing to rest for five minutes after every 15 as we were both feeling tired. We made it into Melrose in the early evening. Melrose has a ruined abbey, reputed to be the final burial place of Robert the Bruce's heart.

We started day 10 for Longformacus, 24 miles away, leaving Melrose by crossing the suspension bridge over the River Tweed, then following the river for some way before heading into farmland. The distance to the small town of Lauder was just 10 miles, the next opportunity to buy more supplies. We decided to push on and left Lauder behind, gaining height into what are known as the Lammermuirs, a vast area of moorland stretching as far as you can see. It started to rain as we crossed this bleak windy moorland, but after some distance, we came across an old barn. Seeking shelter and a break from the weather, Graham pushed open the door only to see rats scurrying for cover everywhere. It was, however, dry, and gave us a chance to rest and have a snack. The short respite was welcome as the wind howled and battered the metal sheets of which the barn was constructed. 15 minutes later, we moved again across the moorland. At the highest point, we encountered two large stone cairns known as The Twin Law Cairns. These were monuments to twin warrior brothers separated at birth who unwittingly fought against each other and died in the battle of Twin Law during Saxon times. A poem dedicated to them was on the cairns. Descending the hill, we encountered more farmland towards Longformacus, crossing several cattle grids. At one grid Graham spotted a tern that had become caught underneath the grid and attempted to rescue it. However, not understanding his kind intention, the bird tried to peck him! Eventually, using a stick, we managed to free it. We found our accommodation, albeit much later then intended, and apologised to the owner who had prepared dinner for us. We were left alone in the property – a lovely family home with a roaring fire – all evening as the owner lived in another part of the village.

Our final day was 18 miles to Cockburnspath, the walk a mixture of farmland and woodland with very little ascent. It was lunchtime when we emerged from woodland and crossed the busy A1 trunk road, gaining our first sight of the North Sea; Pease Bay was soon in view. We turned inland to our destination – the war memorial in the centre of Cockburnspath. Graham had arranged for Nicola, his then girlfriend, to meet us. We had arrived a little ahead of schedule but soon Nicola appeared with a bottle of champagne to celebrate our achievement. We had walked 212 miles diagonally from the west to the east across Scotland's southern uplands in 11 days. There were highs and lows, but, as father and son, we had a great time together.

The years following saw a growth in walking, with better footwear and waterproof clothing inspiring more long-distance paths to be created. In early 2014, I discussed with Kate about doing the Ayrshire coastal path after Trevor and David had given me the guidebook as a 70th birthday present. This path follows the coast from Glenapp in the south to Skelmorlie in the north, a total distance of 94 miles.

Travelling by train and bus to the starting point, we set off on 19 May from Glenapp and covered 45 miles, as far as the town of Ayr. Using pre-booked B&Bs along the way, we had a fantastic time together, seeing some amazing scenery as the path follows the cliffs along the coast before dropping down to the seashore whenever possible. As well as walking, we took as much as time possible to see the historical features along the way. It was a glorious week weatherwise, too. We finished in Ayr, partly due to time constraints and partly because it generated a poignant memory of the holiday we had shared together at the Butlin's holiday camp in 1962. It was still a holiday camp but no longer run by the same company.

On the opposite side of the River Forth from Edinburgh is what is known as the Kingdom of Fife. A long-distance path along this coastline was created in 2002 and runs from Kincardine to Newburgh, totalling 113 miles. In 2016, Paul gave us a gift of a two-night stay at a luxury hotel beside this coast, so Kate and I decided to use the time to explore part of this path. Once again, we experienced the beauty of Scotland and its stunning scenery, the unique topography here very different from the Ayrshire coast. We walked the stretch over three days, from East Wemyss to St. Monans, returning to the same hotel each evening.

The island of Guernsey in the Channel Islands had been our holiday destination in the 1960s and 1970s when Kate's parents lived there; we had spent three weeks every summer on the many beaches around the island. It is an island of beautiful cliff walks too, with spectacular scenery. In 1980, in memory of Kate's parents, we purchased the first ever timeshare on the island. Every first week of September we would return, recalling fond family memories and walking the coastal paths. In 2013, we decided it would be an achievement to walk around the island, keeping close to the coast as much as possible. The distance is approximately 45 miles. We completed this in stages over three years, each year walking in a clockwise direction. Upon completion, the following year, 2017, we decided to walk the route again, this time anticlockwise. It was a wonderful experience viewing the whole island from a different perspective. Each year we would do a section each day and then return the following year to continue until it was complete.

Another wonderful walking country we enjoyed was Madeira, where Kate and I had spent every November since just before the Millenium. Once the clocks went back on the last weekend in October, it was time to escape Scotland, the daylight hours restricted to eight hours, or even less. We both loved Madeira, with its warm climate and walks that follow the Levadas. These are water channels that date back 600 years when early settlers made them to bring water from the mountains and rainforest down to the terraces where all the crops were grown. The paths beside the Levadas and through tunnels total 1,800 miles. We ticked off many recognised walks just by using a local guidebook and map rather than joining an organised walking group.

Walking remains one of my great passions in life; I still have my TRIMARC friends for the mountains, though these are done at a much lower altitude than in the past. I also have local friends who accompany me for the many local walks around Dunblane on recognised routes, many of which are on closed railway tracks.

CONCLUSION

The idea of recording some of my life stories first came to me while on holiday in Madeira 15 years ago.

I have lived through, and witnessed, vast changes in my 80-plus years, the scale of which is unlikely to be seen or experienced by future generations. From living standards to technological advancement, I have been a part of it all, and I wanted to record it for posterity.

My initial intention for the book was to act as a reminder for future generations of my own family, but after friends had read a draft copy, I was persuaded to publish it for a general readership.

I wish my parents had recorded details of their lives; I only have the memories of what they told me: how my mother, the second youngest of 17 children, used to stand on a stool to help my grandmother wash clothes by hand at a sink with no hot running water; my dad volunteering for the war effort by joining the RAF in 1940. How many more precious stories could we have learned if only they had written them down?

I chose to write the things that most mattered to me and recorded my life stories chapter by short chapter: childhood, education, work, sport, hobbies, and of course family. I have also attached an appendix of my hospital admissions to show that no matter how many times adversity strikes, if you have a positive mental attitude, you will always bounce back.

'Failure cannot live with persistence.'

I played sport to win, always within the rules of the game. Though winning isn't everything, it's the only thing if you are competitive! My strive for business success came from not always accepting the status quo; being prepared to challenge the higher authority when I believed they were wrong. There have been times, of course, when I too may have been wrong. I tried to balance family life with all my interests and will forever be grateful to my late wife, Kate, who was an inspiration and support to me for all 56 years of our marriage. My three children have the same work ethic as Kate and I; so too our five grandchildren.

Those friends I have kept in touch with during my journey from Cheveley to Dunblane are still very important to me, especially since my wife's passing. I try to return to Cheveley at least once a year to catch up with friends there, as well as my brother and sister. The village I remember as a lad has hardly changed, still thatched cottages and a rural peaceful way of life.

You cannot count time, but you can make time count.

APPENDIX 1

Medical Operation History

1968 (Nov) – Fractured tibia and fibula (right leg) while playing football.
Newmarket General Hospital – 5 days inpatient – General Anaesthetic (GA)

1972 – Cortisone injections to left elbow for lateral epicondylitis (tennis elbow).
Newmarket General Hospital – Day patient

1978 – Medial meniscectomy to left knee (torn cartilage removal).
Evelyn Nursing Home, Cambridge – 2 days inpatient – GA

1999 (May) – Left inguinal hernia mesh repair.
Kings Park Hospital, Stirling – 2 days inpatient – GA

2003 (Dec) – Tendon surgery for split rotator cuff (left shoulder).
Ross Hall Hospital, Glasgow – 2 days inpatient – GA

2004 (July) – Excision of eight sebaceous cysts.
Kings Park Hospital, Stirling – Day patient – Local Anaesthetic (LA)

2008 (June) – Lesion removal (benign viral wart) from left forearm.
Bannockburn Health Centre – Day patient – LA

2009 (Sept) – Multiple arthroscopic procedures on left knee.
Kings Park Hospital, Stirling – Day patient – GA

2012 (Dec) – Photodynamic therapy to remove basal cell carcinoma from chest.
Kings Park Hospital, Stirling – Day patient – LA

2013 (July) – Excision of basal cell carcinoma from chest.
Kings Park Hospital, Stirling – Day patient – LA

2015 (March) – Brain surgery to decompress trigeminal nerve (left side).
Western General Hospital, Edinburgh – 6 days inpatient – GA

2016 (July) – Cardioversion procedure for irregular heartbeat.
Forth Valley Royal Hospital, Larbert – Day patient – GA

2017 (Feb) – Ablation of left atrial tachycardia.
Spire Shawfair Park Hospital, Edinburgh – 1 day inpatient – Sedation

2018 (Oct) – Open mesh repair of right inguinal hernia.
Kings Park Hospital, Stirling – Day patient – GA

2019 (Dec) – Trans-radial styloid peri-lunate surgery (left wrist fracture from fall).
Forth Valley Royal Hospital, Larbert – 2 days inpatient – GA

2020 (Feb) – Removal of K-wires from left wrist.
Kings Park/Forth Valley Hospital, Larbert – Day patient – GA

2020 (Aug) – Carpal tunnel release (right hand).
Kings Park Hospital, Stirling – Day patient – LA

2020 (Oct) – Removal of basal cell carcinoma from chest.
Forth Valley Royal Hospital, Larbert – Day patient – LA

2021 (Feb) – Left total knee replacement (cemented).
Spire Murrayfield Hospital, Edinburgh – 3 days inpatient – GA

2022 (Dec) – Right total hip replacement (hybrid).
Spire Murrayfield Hospital, Edinburgh – 3 days inpatient – GA

2024 (Apr) – Cataract removal surgery (right eye).
Kings Park Hospital, Stirling – Day patient – LA

2024 (Nov) – Corneal tissue donor graft (right eye).
Moorfields Eye Hospital, London – Day patient – LA

2025 (Sept) – Cataract removal surgery (left eye).
Moorfields Eye Hospital, London – Day patient – LA

GA = General Anaesthetic LA = Local Anaesthetic

APPENDIX 2

Properties I Have Lived In

1943 – 1947
Warren Stud Cottage, Cheveley
Birthplace – Parents' home

1947 – Sept 1952
Great Barton Stud Cottage, Great Barton
Parents' home

1952 – Dec 1953
Dellar Cottage, High Street, Cheveley
Parents' home

1953 – 1961
No. 1 Sandwich Stud Cottage, Cheveley
Parents' home

1961 – June 1964
No. 3 White Lodge Stud Cottage, Cheveley
Parents' home

1964 – August 1964
38 Ashley Road, Newmarket
In-laws' home

1964 – January 1976
12 Heathbell Road, Newmarket
Our 1st home together
Purchased: £3,250 | Sold: £12,600

1976 – April 1980
25 Elizabeth Avenue, Newmarket
Our 2nd home
Purchased: £13,950 | Sold: £15,750

1980 – July 1981
117 London Road North, Poynton, Cheshire
Our 3rd home
Purchased: £48,000 | Sold: £48,000

1981 – Oct 2006
The Arns Cottage, Dunblane
Our 4th home
Purchased: £49,000 | Sold: £295,000

2006 – Present
Gleniffer, Doune Road, Kilbryde, Dunblane
Our 5th home
Purchased: £485,266

Printed in Dunstable, United Kingdom

72376607R00147